Title: Together, They Faced Hell
Author: Sally E Cox
ISBN: 978-0-6458923-7-6

Together, They Faced Hell is based on the bond between the young men of the Light Horse and their horses in the Desert Campaign of WW1.

©Sally E Cox 2023
All rights reserved. No part of this book may be reproduced or transmitted in any form or by any means, electronic or mechanical, including photocopying, recording or by any information storage and retrieval system, without prior permission in writing from the author.
Contact: sally57e@gmail.com

Editing and design
PB Publishing
Gisborne Victoria
www.pbpublishing.com.au

Printed in Australia

 A catalogue record for this book is available from the National Library of Australia

Front cover: Painting 'A Drop for My Mate'
©Ron Marshall
www.lighthorseart.com.au

Dedication

**'Most obediently, often most painfully, they died,
faithful unto death.'**

To the brave Lighthorsemen and their loyal horses who faced untold traumas in the Desert Campaign WW1. We honour you.

To the nearly one million horses who died during World War 1.

To my daughter, Elizabeth (Lizze) who showed me the incredible bond between a girl and her horse and the complete trust a horse will place in their owner even when both are trembling with fear.

To Pony Club Australia for promoting equestrian events which cater for the thousands of young horse lovers. To the mounted games competition which requires stunning riding skills, accurate hand-eye co-ordination, teamwork, athleticism and a fast pony. These skills were undoubtedly displayed by the Light Horsemen.

To Sporting Horse Australia for providing competitions beyond pony club, which require the many skills demonstrated in the mounted games.

To the young country boys aged between 19 and 21 (many were under-age) who believed the advertising for the war as an event of patriotism, comradeship, adventure, sport and good fun. They signed up with their horses: 'Those starry-eyed young men and frightened horses who went off to war.'

To Maxwell Christian Curwen-Walker, my grandfather's cousin, 23/5th Light Horse Regiment. Queensland. The best from Queensland who fought in all the battles since Gallipoli.

Surely the bond of love and trust between man and animal was essential in the war, where death and terror were constant companions. The amazing riding ability of the young men in the Light Horse can be fully appreciated by the acknowledgement of the incredible contribution of the horses who endured heat, thirst, injury, fear and deprivation with their riders. Together they were a magnificent force, joined by love and trust.

It was a tragedy for these young, enthusiastic men and their beloved horses who, together, faced Hell. While survivors returned home, none of the horses did except for one, Sandy.

Acknowledgements

A special thank you to Phillipa Butler, my editor, who liked the idea I shared with her, refining my writing and for finding many of the images that I needed.

The inspiration for writing this book was my daughter, Lizze and her passion for horses. I watched as she and her teammates competed in the pony club mounted games over the years. Skill and a partnership between horse and rider were essential. Her team won at state level and it was exciting to be part of that. My son, Mark, also joined the games team and he and Lizze had great fun competing. They both loved their horses.

At a Sporting Horse competition day, a particular event, the Rescue Relay will forever remain embedded in my memory. Lizze had to race her pony, Storm, a little 13-hand Welsh mountain pony to collect her rescue person, Teegan, who had to jump on the back and then race back to the finish line with both on board. They won and their excitement was priceless. Much later when I was researching for my book, I read the account of 'Bill the Bastard' rescuing the four troopers from the desert at Romani and I could imagine little Storm doing that as he had courage and stamina.

Lizze Cox on Storm, competing in the Mounted Games.

To my daughter's friend Mathew Slade, who drowned on 9 January 1913, aged 21, while in New Zealand preparing for the World Team Mounted Games Championships. He epitomised the young, enthusiastic and adventurous young man who loved life and his horses, much like those young men who joined the Light Horse.

I need to thank my husband, John, and my mother, Mayzod, who encouraged me. Sadly, my mum passed away in 2019. Both have a gentle, loving way with horses. John has had to put up with the many hours I spent deep in the incredible journey by man and his horse in a hostile environment.

Thank you to my teacher friends at school, Tracey, Ann, Robbo and Angela Chau, who kept asking me how my writing was going and kept encouraging me.

I was moved by the lovely people who answered my requests for information about their relatives who joined the Light Horse.

I am indebted to Gloria Auchterlonie who welcomed me into her home to talk about her efforts printing her father-in-law's diary. She has donated her collection of his records, photos and diaries to the State Library. She is an inspirational woman who had a remarkable story to tell about finding Trooper George Auchterlonie's diaries, letters and photos in a tin trunk on her farm. I have mentioned him in the book.

To Ron and Jennifer Marshall for their beautiful lighthorse paintings which depict powerful images of the horses, their riders, their bond and the incredible feats they achieved together.

I am grateful for the work of Trooper Ion I. Idriess, for his detailed writing while being involved in the Desert Campaign. I used many quotes from his book *The Desert Column*. This book was loved by my father, who gave me his copy.

To Roland Perry for his thorough research into an amazing war horse, *Bill the Bastard*. His book was inspirational and reinforced my belief in the amazing bond between man and horse during WWI when horses were crucial to success in the Desert Campaign.

I am grateful for the many references and images used in this publication, from many sources including the Australian War Memorial. The pictures give potency to the words.

Our lives are richer for having the privilege of caring for and sharing our lives with horses.
'His horse is more than a friend, he is part of the soldier's very life.'
—Lt-Col C. Guy Powles

The Horse Holder by Ron Marshall

Artworks by kind permission Ron and Jennifer Marshall, Light Horse Art, Queensland.

Best Mates by Jennifer Marshall

'His horse is more than a friend, he is part of the soldier's very life.'

Night Stunt by Ron Marshall

Commiseration by Jennifer Marshall

Author's Note

The horses' untold story during World War 1

Every year when we honour the ANZACS at various parades and services, we think about the huge sacrifices made by the soldiers and their families, particularly during the First World War when tens of thousands of young men lost their lives. They endured horrific conditions at Gallipoli, on the Western Front and in the harsh deserts of the Middle East. In large part they were 'swamped by power and technology" But do we ever consider the plight of the trusted horses who, with their riders, also faced the traumas of war? The horses were sent halfway round the world to face conditions so appalling that man and horse must have been united in their terror. But these horses boosted morale and allowed a sense of humanity for the men, who could comfort and care for another living creature in an environment of destruction and death.

Many of the enthusiastic young men who joined the Light Horse Brigade in World War I were either killed or maimed, physically, emotionally, or both. At least half of the Light Horse was initially made up of young men aged between 19 and 21, the 'boys' army', while the other half was made up of experienced soldiers. Those who returned were scarred by the experiences of war; of having seen their mates die, and watching their faithful horses sink in the mud in Europe or die from horrendous wounds. Others endured heat, sand and thirst in the desert campaigns of the Middle East. Of those who survived the war, many planned to buy their horses from the army but were told that, because of quarantine regulations, it was impractical to ship thousands of army horses back to Australia. While thousands of the horses were sold in Britain and India, those considered too old for sale were put down, and many were sold in Egypt to be beasts of burden: to haul heavy loads in the streets of Cairo or toil in quarries and mines for owners who were too poor to feed them properly. For some soldiers this prospect was too much, they would rather shoot their horse, their friend, than leave him to this cruel fate. Instead of being treated with the respect a soldier deserved, these war horses were discarded and left behind.

This story is first and foremost a tribute to the great bond between horse and man sent into the hell of WW1.

The Light Horsemen rode Walers, a rugged animal that began its development in the very early years of Australian colonial history. The history of the breed began with the arrival of the First Fleet which, brought the first horses to Australia in 1788. These were of English thoroughbred and Spanish stock. Later importations included more thoroughbreds, Arabs and Timor and Welsh Mountain ponies. The Australian Stock Horse evolved through selective breeding in response to the demands of the environment. It was in the mid-1800s, following a boom in demand from other countries for the Australian-bred horse, that the Waler earnt its name—the term 'Waler' being a nickname coined by the British to describe the Australian horses being imported through New South Wales. "Strong and great-hearted with strains of thoroughbred and semi-draught to give them speed, strength and stamina," was one description.

The horses that went to war were not recorded with names, only brands and numbers—each horse was branded with the Government broad arrow and initials of the purchasing officer, and an army number on one hoof—but their characters were known well by their owners who gave them epithets like 'Bill the Bastard', 'Wrinkle Bum,' and 'Sulky Sam.'

A.B. 'Banjo' Paterson, the Australian poet and passionate horse lover who raised the profile of war horses, wrote, "the horse was a mate. Through the suffering and deprivation, a bond developed between man and beast, a feeling of affection and trust—a real partnership." J.M. Brereton wrote in his book, *The Horse in War*, "the soldier came to regard his horse almost as an extension of his own being". Jill, Duchess of Hamilton, in her book *First to Damascus*, published a photo of her father, Private Noel Robertson, on his warhorse but she never knew the horse's name. Her father would be "overcome with emotion at my mention of his horse," she wrote. He rarely spoke of him. He had been forced to kill the creature he loved so much, and he never recovered from having to shoot his beloved horse. Looking at the photo of her father and his horse, she commented, "In the photo, the horse is as important as the rider. Take away the horse and the picture shows nothing. The animal gives potency to the rider."

An article in *Kia Ora Coo-ee* (the Anzacs' wartime magazine in the Middle East) of 15 December 1918 titled "Mulga", conveys the great love between one trooper, 'Big Jim', and the horse he had chosen at the remount depot called 'Mulga'. "Sometimes his mates would tease him about that love where Jim would lay shivering on the freezing nights of lonely patrols and give his saddle blanket to Mulga...Mulga was killed when making an advance on Damascus and Jim had a shattered knee.

"Jim is home now and the folks there are often puzzled at an indefinable something missing from his sunny nature; and Jim, being reticent, probably they won't know. But his troop mates will tell you that half the laughter left his eyes, half the lightness his voice, that day when he left the brown horse, Mulga, lying so weirdly still on the battle-scarred sward of a Syrian plain."

It was a testament to the powerful bond between a man and his horse that Major-General Sir William Bridges, first Commandant of the Military College at Duntroon, Canberra, and the first Commander-in-Chief of the Australian Imperial Forces, ordered that his warhorse, companion and mate, 'Sandy', be returned to Australia. Sandy had been sold to the Army at the outbreak of war and Bridges had noticed him at training and wanted him for his mount. They spent time together in Egypt until Bridges went to Gallipoli on 25 April 1915. Unfortunately, a month later, Major-General Bridges was killed by a sniper's bullet. He was the only Australian killed in WW1 to have his remains returned to Australia. He was buried at Duntroon. Sandy, his horse, in line with Bridges' wishes, was also brought home to Australia, the only Australian horse to be returned. Private Archibald Jordan, who had been hospitalised since April 1917 as permanently unfit, accompanied Sandy in September 1918 on his journey to Melbourne, arriving in November 1918.

Similarly, Colonel Guy Powles from the New Zealand Mounted Rifles was together with his mount, Bess, for the entire desert campaign. His horse and three others were saved. They went to France for quarantine and then to England. Powles rode Bess in the Victory Parades down the streets of Berlin.

This story is also about the men who joined the Light Horse Brigade; those who "with neither a bridle nor the crucial bit, ... could turn a horse by tapping on its neck"[1]; the station hands, the drovers and the many young farm boys. There were also the Remounts, who were sent to train and look after the horses. A.B. 'Banjo' Paterson was sent to the British base at Maadi in Egypt in December 1915. He was later made Chief Officer of the newly combined Remount Unit at the huge British base at Moascar, outside Cairo. Paterson was responsible for buying replacement horses for the army, and many of these horses could be rough and difficult to handle. One of the worst examples of a difficult handler was a horse called Jezebel. She was described as "a tall, rangy brute with ... the sourest nature ever implanted in a horse,"[2] who upset a whole squadron. Trooper 'Snow' Matson was assigned Jezebel. Snow was a good horseman but he could not build

1 Jill Duchess of Hamilton – *The Story of The Light Horse and Lawrence of Arabia*, ... p25

2 *A Story About a Horse Called Jezebel*, as told to R S Porteous – www.lighthorse.org.au

a rapport with the mare. If he brushed her flanks or tried to do up her girth, she would kick out or bite him. She would kick and bite horses on either side of her. At mounted parades she would fidget around and not stand still and on long rides would proceed in an uncomfortable jig-jog rather than walk. Like many of the horses she hated camels, and would bolt at the sight of them. Camels were crucial to the desert assault and while most of the horses gradually became used to them, Jezebel did not. She was eventually killed by a shell and Snow Matson was assigned another horse, much to his relief.

There were also older men, too old for the brigade—jackaroos, horse breakers, ex-jockeys, buck-jumping riders and vets—there to train and look after the horses used in the army while the soldiers were fighting in Gallipoli. They all have stories to tell about the strength and beauty of these incredible horses.

> **136,000 horses were sent from Australia for the war effort until 1917 and only one returned home.**
>
> **11,000 horses were sent from New Zealand and only four returned home.**
>
> **It has been said of the bond between man and horse that, "One is no good without the other."**

The men of the Light Horse were sent as reinforcements to Gallipoli during 1915 and were thus forced to part with their beloved horses, as horses were little used at Gallipoli. Many had brought their own horses from their farms and had a relationship of affection and trust with them. It was heartbreaking for the men, and their horses would have suffered from the absence of their familiar owners.

There were 136,000 horses sent from Australia for the war effort until 1917 and only one returned home. From New Zealand, 11,000 horses were sent and only four returned home. It has been said of the bond between man and horse that, "One is no good without the other."

While the New Zealand contribution was less in number, the bravery of the soldiers and their love for their horses equalled the Australians', and both received little recognition in the British press. In fact, the ANZACS were known as 'devils on horses' by the Turks because "they never knew where they would strike next. The Turks' reconnaissance planes would report no movement in the enemy camps at sundown, yet by daybreak the ANZACS would be attacking a position 20 miles away from their base, which the Turks had never thought possible," quoted Terry Kinloch in his 2007 book *Devils on Horses*. The war horses were the unsung heroes of the hell called World War One.

Contents

Introduction • 1

Maps 1. Area map during WW1 where the Light Horse were used to capture Palestine and Syria from Turkish control. • 3
      2. The Light Horse campaign from Egypt to Syria • 4

Chapter 1   Background to the Light Horse • 5

Chapter 2   The men who joined the Light Horse • 8

Chapter 3   Conditions on board ship • 14

Chapter 4   Training in Egypt: The Remount Depots • 16

Chapter 5   Conditions on the Western Front • 34

Chapter 6   The Light Horse in the Middle East • 41

Chapter 7   The push to Palestine, 1917 • 61

Chapter 8   Beersheba: 31 October 1917 • 70

Chapter 9   The push north: November 1917–January 1918 • 79

Chapter 10 The Great Ruse: September 1918, Syria • 90

Chapter 11 The Great Ride: 19 September–1 October 1918 • 96

Chapter 12 Damascus and the end of the war • 99

Chapter 13 What happened to the horses? • 103

Chapter 14 Conclusion • 112

Chapter 15 Tributes to the horses • 117

Chapter 16 Some horses mentioned • 128

Chapter 17 Memorials • 135

Appendix: Who's who in leadership • 145

Glossary • 148

Timeline of Middle East Campaign • 152

Light Horse formations and leaders • 154

Regiments and troopers mentioned • 157

Bibliography • 158

Image courtesy family of Esmond Lecchi

Pals: a trooper and his horse share a tender moment.

Introduction

In 1914 when WW1 broke out, Egypt was a province of the Turkish Ottoman Empire but had been under British rule for more than thirty years. When Turkey entered the war siding with Germany, the Suez Canal was important to both England and Turkey for movement of troops and trade between England, India, Australia and New Zealand. In 1915, there was a boundary about 150 kilometres east of the Suez Canal between Egyptian Sinai and the Ottoman-controlled Palestine. It stretched from Rafa (near the Mediterranean coast) to Akaba on the Red Sea. The Turkish army had tried to take control of the Suez but the desert was too harsh and was a formidable obstacle. Troops from the British Empire were stationed in Egypt to guard the Suez Canal. The Desert Campaign (1916–1918) was important to push the Turks from Egypt, then capture Palestine and Syria from Turkish rule (which had been in place over 600 years.) This was necessary as the Turks had been freed from Gallipoli by December 1915 and had sent reinforcements to the Middle East. Ion Idriess (5th Regiment Light Horse) in his book *The Desert Column*, commented, "We, our outpost, are really guarding the 100 miles of waterway with its load of ships…If we lose, England loses the Canal and all the army in Egypt…So the lives of hundreds and thousands of men might well rest on this sun-browned outpost gazing away out across the desert."

The Anzac Mounted Division was formed in May 1916 after the abandonment of Gallipoli, with Major-General Harry Chauvel as leader. He was "an easy-going natural leader…reserved and aloof in manner, gentle of speech and quiet of bearing," recorded the official Australian War Historian for the Sinai and Palestine, Henry Gullet.

Orders were to send a Mounted Division of the AIF—the Light Horse—to cross the hostile desert. The Light Horse was so named because they were a mounted Infantry without heavy weapons such as swords. They worked in sections (four men to a section.) They carried only a rifle with a bayonet because the strategy was that they would gallop up, dismount, one soldier would hold the four horses and take them to safety while the other three fought, then they would all retreat and make a fast getaway.

How could a mounted division cross a hostile desert?
1. English engineers and Egyptian labour created a railway line and a water pipe from the Suez Canal at Kantara across the Sinai Desert into Turkish Palestine. Water was essential to survival.
2. The Camel Corps, 'the trucks of the desert,' carried food, water and supplies.
3. Excellent Australian horses and bush soldiers.
4. Night patrols where they could leave quickly, fully armed, mounted and ready to go.

Obstacles
1. Lack of water, hunger and lack of sleep.
2. Sand, storms and searing heat.
3. German planes would target horses on 'tied' lines. Many were killed. Soldiers would try to release them into the desert and scatter making them a difficult target. They would often make dummy horse lines to combat this problem.
4. Attacks from snipers and ambush.

Why the Light Horse?
1. A form of rapid transport — mounted infantry and talented horses. The Light Horse was not cavalry, but a highly mobile, mounted infantry.
2. Used for reconnaissance — they would ride ahead to check out the whereabouts of Turkish troops.
3. Efficient fighting force. They had audacity, could dash, had courage and endurance.
4. The Light Horse matched the Bedouin's ability to survive and thrive in the desert.
5. The partnership between man and horse was more than trust and devotion; they shared a sense of mutual dependency. The importance of working in 'Sections' is not to be overlooked—four men living together, sleeping, and potentially dying together.
6. The Light Horsemen were used to the self-sufficient outdoor life, using firearms, navigation skills and using their initiative.

How did they succeed?
It was a patient conquest of the Sinai, Palestine and Syria through lonely, long-range patrolling by the Light Horse, bloody and persistent battles, brilliant leadership, support by the Camel Corps and New Zealand Mounted Rifles, perseverance, initiative and humour. It also needed the British and Australian planes scouring the area, great engineering and the amazing partnership between man and horse.

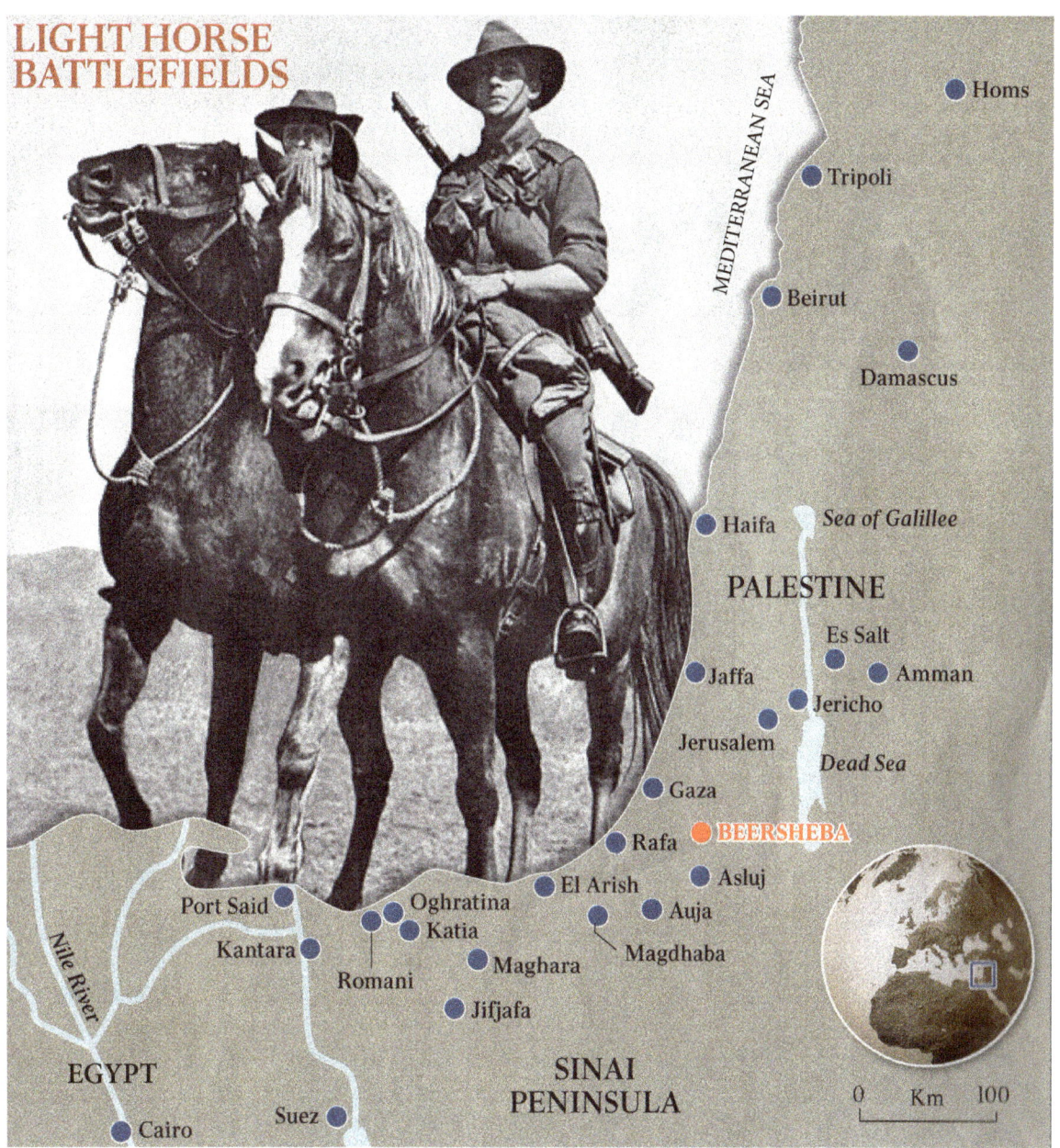

Light Horse battlefields in the Sinai and Palestine in the Desert Campaign.

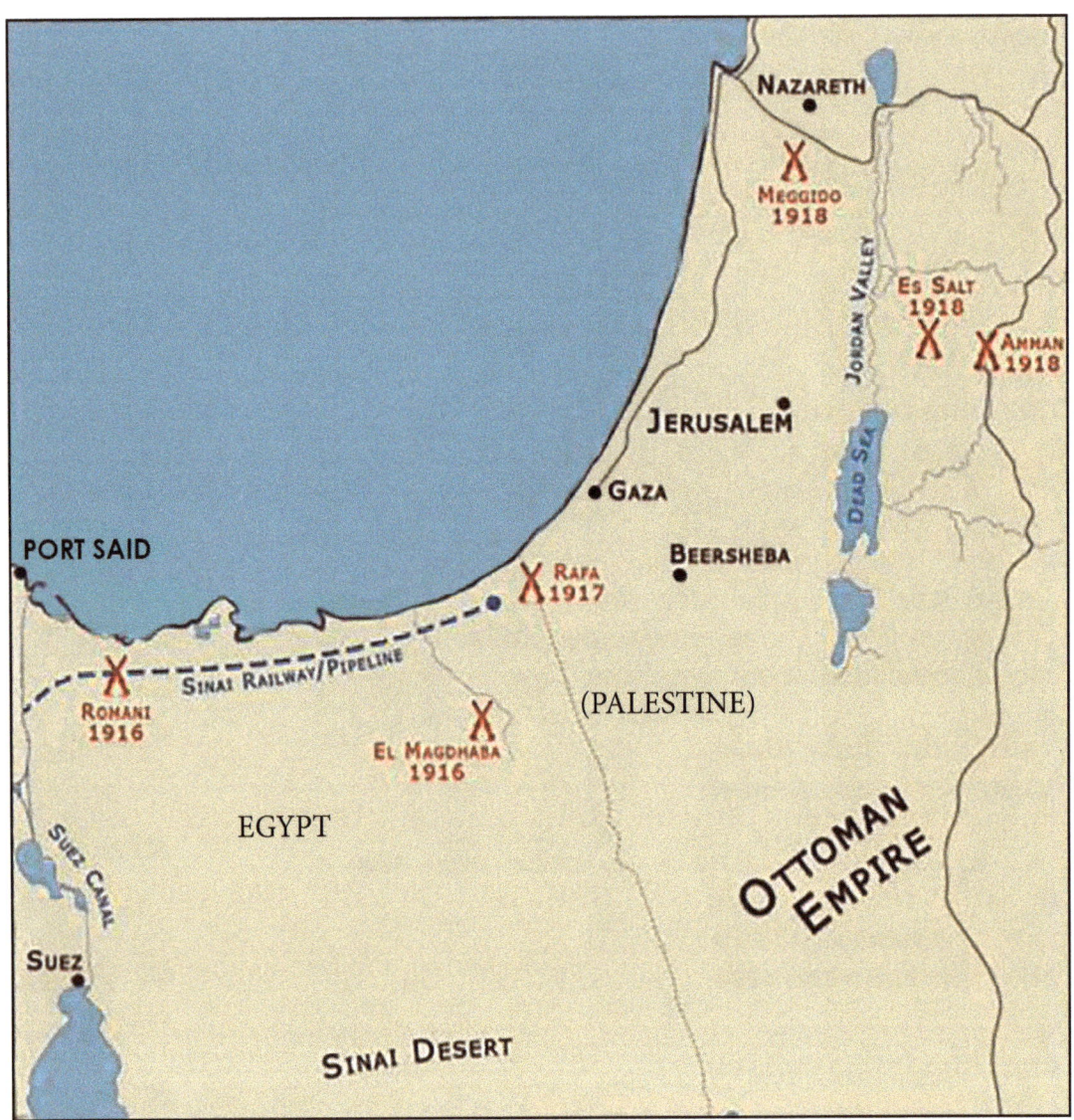

Light Horse campaign from Egypt to Syria, map also shows route of the railway and pipeline constructed during the war, and some battles of the Light Horse through Sinai, Palestine and the Jordan Valley.

1
Background to the Light Horse

'We needed to be able to defend ourselves'

Australian mounted citizen soldier forces were originally formed around the mid-19th century, when the need was seen for a local, home-grown defence force. There was unrest, such as that caused by mining taxes which resulted in the Eureka Stockade in Ballarat, Victoria, in 1854, and a fear of Russian invasion around that time. Three states, NSW, Victoria and South Australia, created their own small cavalry forces. It became tradition for mounted citizen soldiers to be men who could ride their own horses and train in their spare time.

In Victoria, the Kyneton Mounted Rifle Corps was formed in 1857 with 100 enlistees. During the 1860s they trained with the Castlemaine Light Dragoons and the Bendigo Volunteer Rifles. In 1863 the Prince of Wales gave permission for the whole Victorian Volunteer Horse troops to become the "Prince of Wales Light Horse". In the 1870s they participated in military gymkhanas and amalgamated into a regiment. The Victorian Mounted Rifles was formed in 1885 and in 1887, the local Seymour branch was formed and began training at Golden Paddocks, four kilometres east of Seymour. The training ground was part of a cattle and sheep run known as Marengo. Seymour was seen as a good place to train because it was relatively close to Melbourne, hilly and had a railway.

In NSW, it was announced in August 1897 that a new military force, the First Australian Volunteer Horse, would be established, and articles and advertisements appeared in local papers. While the headquarters would be in Sydney, recruiting would only be carried out in the country. The Harden-Murrumburrah district was chosen as one of the main recruitment centres and a muster was held at the Murrumburrah racecourse on 30 August. About 100 horsemen turned up, attracted by the promise of comradeship, sport and good fun. Sixty men were chosen, those being the most competent riders with their own horses. The uniform for the unit was myrtle green with a black cock's plume in their hat. They became one of the founding units which made up the Australian Light Horse when all the troops were amalgamated in 1903 as a result of Federation, and their nickname was the 'Irish Guard'.

The second Boer War in South Africa broke out in 1899. About thirty of the recruits from Harden-Murrumburrah went to this war. They and other local troops were non-professional colonial cavalrymen and the British were reluctant to use them, yet they proved to be more than a match for the fast-moving mounted commandoes of the Boers as they were expert rough-riding horsemen, good shots and bush-hardened.

Recreated troopers uniform of the First Australian Volunteer Horse.

They were unconventional and did not follow the British tradition of charging in—the 'noble death and glory' tradition—but rather fought against the odds by ambush and stealth. These tactics would be used in the desert warfare by the Light Horse later in WW1. The tradition of 'noble death and glory' was to become evident later in WW1 at Gallipoli and in the trenches and battlefields of France and Belgium. What it really meant, however, was the continued use of 19th century tactics against 20th century technology, where it became no longer 'honour' and 'bravery', charging at the enemy in face-to-face combat but 'slaughter,' the men facing rapid-fire machine guns.

In Queensland, in response to fears expressed by the Governor that the two principal towns of the colony, Brisbane and Ipswich, would be defenceless in the case of a hostile action, the Queensland Light Horse was formed in the 1860s, though this volunteer force did not gain great numbers through the next decades. The uniform was khaki with claret-coloured facings, and the members wore emu plumes in their hats. Each man provided his own horse and received a horse allowance. In 1899, Queensland sent three contingents of volunteers from what was then called the Queensland Mounted Infantry to the Boer War.

Uniform worn by a member of the 6th Light Horse, Trooper S J Crozier of Queensland.

A current-day soldier wears the Australian Light Horse uniform.

A small voluntary militia formed in South Australia with a modest force of militia and some cavalry. In 1870, because of the Franco-Prussian war in France, the force was reorganised into two battalions, two artillery batteries and four troops of cavalry. By 1899 the first contingent of SA Mounted Rifles was formed and by 1900, the second contingent served in the second Boer War. Among its men was Lance-Corporal Harry Morant (Breaker Morant, executed for killing civilians during his service). In 1901, Australia became a Federation and the colonial armies were united to form the Commonwealth Military Forces.

In 1903 the Australian Light Horse (ALH) was formed and the First Australian Volunteer Horse was absorbed into the ALH. By 1909, compulsory military training was legislated and a month after war was declared in July 1914, the Australian Imperial Force was formed, which included 23 Light Horse Regiments from around the country.

2
The men who joined the Light Horse
'Comradeship, sport and good fun'

Why did so many young men from the country flock to join the Light Horse? When the call for volunteers was issued, the response was overwhelming. Young boys from the bush aged 19 to 21, who could ride, shoot and survive in the bush, saw their chance to prove their courage, manhood and patriotism. The advertising seeking volunteers for World War 1 emphasised comradeship, adventure, sport and good fun. The combination of a great adventure, a chance to go overseas and loyalty to the British Empire was further bolstered by the belief that they would be home by Christmas.

They did not know the true nature of what they would face. Children had learned at school stories of heroic deeds and the British Empire and heard stories of the Boer War, where soldiers could prove their courage, charging the enemy on horseback. 'Riding for glory and noble death' was a concept long portrayed in English history. The young men signed up for adventure and could not possibly know that they would face bullets, bombs and carnage on a scale never before seen in history. This generation respected authority and was taught to follow orders, and they obeyed no matter how suicidal the commands seemed. They obeyed with the spirit described in Tennyson's chilling line in his poem, *The Charge of the Light Brigade*:

> "Theirs is not to reason why,
> Theirs but to do or die."

In 1910, compulsory military training was introduced in Australia and the home defence militia—the Commonwealth Military Force—was formed. A training camp was conducted at Seymour in January 1910 while the British military chief, Lord Kitchener, was in Australia to inspect the Commonwealth's defence preparedness. Four thousand soldiers and two thousand horses trained and took part in military manoeuvres at Seymour racecourse to impress Kitchener, with half being young men in the Infantry and Light Horse (nicknamed the Boys' Army).

When World War I broke out in 1914, General Bridges saw the need to form a new army. It was called the Australian Imperial Force (AIF), with half being the young men of the Light Horse and the other half being men who had served in other wars. First Nations men were not allowed to join because, in the unfortunate attitudes of the time, they were not of European descent and were not considered citizens. Later, in 1917, people of mixed FIrst Nations-European heritage could enlist because there was a shortage of volunteers. First Nations men in the 11th Light Horse Regiment, Queensland, were known as the 'Queensland black watch' in the Jordan Valley.

By 1914, the newly formed AIF was ready to respond to the call to war. Some Light Horsemen took their own horses while others broke in new mounts. They looked impressive in their hats with emu plumes. The use of emu plumes in slouch hats started with the Queensland Mounted Infantry in the 1890s. They tested their skills racing after wild emus. When they caught one at a gallop, they would pull out a couple of the terrified bird's chest feathers and proudly tuck them into their hat bands. They became a symbol of the Australian Light Horse and were nicknamed 'kangaroo feathers.'

The Light Horse called themselves 'Billjims,' reflecting their ordinariness—Bill and Jim were common names. Many of the young men were expert riders, being station hands, farm boys and drovers. The bush life had hardened and prepared them for difficult conditions, to survive for long periods with little water and food. With them in the regiments were soldiers who had fought in the Boer War who provided experience and war skills.

The horses used by the Light Horse were known as Walers, a tough Arab-cross with strong necks and backs, small hooves, and generally standing 14 to 16 hands high. Most of the early Walers carried thoroughbred blood, with some recorded as race winners. They were suited to the harsh desert climate, capable of great endurance even when under extreme stress from lack of food and water. They also had speed and agility. As a cavalry mount, the Waler was ideal because it could maintain a fast walk and progress directly to a steady, level canter without resorting to an uncomfortable trot.

The Light Horse uniform consisted of an AIF jacket, cord riding breeches, leather puttee leggings bound by a spiral strap, slouch hat, and a leather bandolier that carried ninety rounds of ammunition.

In late 1914 there were four Light Horse regiments, 600 men in each. The riders

TOGETHER THEY FACED HELL

Above: Battle-ready Light Horse trooper sans emu plume. In the beginning, only Queensland troopers wore the feathers. Below: Regulation boots, stiff leather puttees and stirrups.

had to provide their own horses which were then purchased by the army and given serial numbers. In early 1915, nine more regiments were added. The thirteen regiments were: 1st from NSW, 2nd from Queensland, 3rd from South Australia, 4th from Victoria, 5th from Queensland, 6th and 7th from NSW, 8th from Victoria, 9th from South Australia and Victoria, 10th from Western Australia, 11th from Queensland and South Australia, 12th from NSW and 13th from Victoria.

The Remount Branch of the Australian Military Forces was set up in 1911-12 in Maribyrnong in Melbourne. Horses were purchased for military training. It was a crucial service to provide fit, trained horses for Australian mounted troops serving in Europe and India. When war was declared in 1914, the Central Remount Depot in Maribyrnong continued its training regimes. Army camps were set up at Broadmeadows and Maribyrnong to train the army recruits from 1914. No birth certificate was needed to enlist. In fact, many boys were younger than 19. They were eager for adventure and to do their duty for the Empire.

The volunteers underwent intensive training and drills. Recruits took a riding test, including having to ride bareback over a water jump, and underwent a strict medical test. Many had their own horses which were bought by the Commonwealth for 30 pounds, and others were issued with remounts. The horses were branded with a government broad arrow and the initials of the purchasing officer and an army number on one hoof. Each morning the trainees fed, watered and groomed their horses, did their training and practised drill and mastery of infantry fighting techniques.

In 1915, the Seymour Camp was a major training centre for the army to build up the AIF, and a main Victorian training area for the Light Horse. It also became an isolation camp to stop the spread of disease such as viral meningitis, which swept through training camps such as Broadmeadows in 1915. Horses were transported to Seymour from distant places by train, jumped from their special carriages and were taken to camp for training. In 1915 there were 15,000 troops training there. Each regiment was set up in four-man sections. In action, three men would dismount and fight as infantry while the fourth man led the horses to cover. After nine weeks the volunteers were allocated their horses and continued their preparations for sailing to England.

Lieutenant-General Harry Chauvel

The commander of the Australian First Light Horse Brigade, Lieutenant-General Harry Chauvel, aged 49, had worked on a cattle station in Queensland. He was an excellent rider and leader. He cared for the horses and his men. With him was a brilliant Lieutenant, Michael

Lieutenant Michael Shanahan, the 'horse whisperer'

Shanahan, 44, who had an uncanny way with animals. A 'horse whisperer,' he spoke softly to the horses and understood them. He had a relaxed, non-threatening manner. The horses responded to suggestion, not bullying.

In October 1914, it was a hive of activity at the Maribyrnong Remount Depot in Victoria. Horses and Light Horsemen were being sent to Station Pier, Port Melbourne, where on October 19 the Wiltshire set sail, followed on October 21 by the HMAT Orvieto, the largest among the first ships to depart Melbourne. Loyalty to the British Empire was the norm at the time, and this was clearly demonstrated in a report from an Australian war correspondent and photographer for *The Age* newspaper, Philip Schuber, who was there to cover the departure of the ships. He was deeply moved as the HMAT

Orvieto set sail: "Never shall I for one (and there were hundreds on board in whose throat a lump arose) forget the sudden quiet on ship and shore as the band played the National Anthem when the liner slowly moved from the pier out into the channel," he wrote.

On board ship were 1500 soldiers, nurses and vets, as well as General Bridges, Harry Chauvel, and the war correspondent and official historian Charles Bean. Bridges' horse, Sandy, was on board with 20 other horses. The convoy leaving Melbourne consisted of 25 Australian ships and 10 New Zealand vessels in the rear. They set sail for Albany, Western Australia, and joined other ships at King George Sound, off Albany. In total this 1st Anzac Convoy was huge, consisting of 40 ships and 8000 horses.

One ship, the Leviathan, was a huge and powerful vessel (named after the biblical sea serpent). Travelling on the Leviathan was A.B. 'Banjo' Paterson, 50, the famous Australian poet and horse lover. Paterson was assigned by *The Sydney Morning Herald* as the paper's "Special Commissioner with the Australian troops," according to his byline. His own horse, 'Trumper,' was a sleek Waler. Also on board was a horse that was to become a hero. He was known as 'Bill the Bastard'. Bill was a huge, 17-hand, 730-kilogram chestnut Waler. He had a gentle and laid-back attitude—until he was ridden. He would allow his rider to mount and then choose his moment to buck fiercely; his independent nature would not allow him to be dominated. In fact, he had not been fully broken in. Many horses that were shipped off had not been fully broken but there were hundreds of trainers being sent to the remount depots in Egypt who would finish the job.

The 1st Convoy left Albany on November 1, 1914. This was an awe-inspiring, historical moment. The Western Australian onlookers would have been excited to see thousands of men and hundreds of horses at the railway station ready to head down to the jetty and board the waiting ships in the harbour at King George Sound. Such a patriotic gathering for King and Country. Paterson wrote,

> "Sunday, November 1st, was a red-letter day in the history of Australia, for on that day our big fleet of transports put out from Albany for the long trip across half the world."
>
> He vividly captured the sight: "The leading vessel draws out past the lighthouse and turns sharply to the West, rising to the lift of the open sea, and as each big vessel clears the gateway of the harbour, she, too, swings round to the west after her leader and seems to dip her head into the waves with a sort of enjoyment at being once more on the trail. As gracefully as a fleet of swans after some great leader, they drop into place and soon are rising to the sea."

Horses wait for loading on to troopship A39 at Port Melbourne in 1915.

His stirring account finishes with,
> "And always behind us are the great towering leviathans of merchantmen, each loaded with men, horses and war material. It is the most wonderful sight that an Australian ever saw."

The New Zealand Mounted Rifles had sailed in October 1914, in time to join the Australian Light Horse convoys. Originally, the Light Horse were to train in England, but Chauvel thought conditions were too severe, it being the northern winter. In addition, Turkey had entered the war on the German side, so the troops were diverted to Egypt to train, protect the Suez Canal and act as a deterrent to Turkey.

In February 1915 a second convoy left Port Philip Bay, Melbourne, with 10,000 troops aboard and thousands of horses, including the 8th Light Horse Regiment. Sailing in this convoy was Colonel (later Sir) John Monash with his horse, Tom, who was described as gentle and well-mannered, strong, willing and responsive.

In total, 136,000 horses were shipped from Australia between 1914 and 1917. No more were sent after January 1917. Remount shipments from New Zealand ceased at the end of 1916.

3
Conditions on board ship
'It was humid, and often dreadful squalls battered the ships'

The trip to Egypt from Albany took four to six weeks. Conditions on board were barely adequate for the men; imagine how cramped and airless conditions must have been for the horses. It was humid, and often dreadful squalls battered the ships. Horses suffered cuts and bruises, colic and pneumonia. The upper deck was well lit and ventilated but the lower decks were dark and poorly ventilated. Food for the horses consisted of oats, bran and chaff. Water was essential, and mucking out the stalls was crucial for the welfare of the horses. Despite the care and attention, horses died due to pneumonia, overcrowding and lack of ventilation on the lowest deck.

The upper deck of a New Zealand transport ship heading to Egypt in 1915 shows the best of conditions that could be hoped for horses.

On the transport the Wiltshire, which set sail on 19 October 1914 from Melbourne to join the convoy sailing from Western Australia, the horses were kept in the stalls the entire time. They fretted, played up, reared and caused themselves severe injuries that sometimes resulted in their deaths. In the convoys there were 50 vessels, 30,000 men and 12,000 horses. The horse handlers fed and watered their charges but the animals were kept locked up. They fretted and were often forced into submission or had blindfolds tied around their eyes. Some handlers knew how to treat them with kindness and coaxing, not the whip and yelling. Where possible, a morning fitness program was set up, after which the horses were groomed. Elyne Mitchell in her book, *Light Horse*, noted that "constant grooming and exercising kept the horses fit…the management of the horses, and the complete dependence of each horse on its owner for water, food and attention, strengthened the bond between man and horse." The horses responded to good treatment on board the ships.

Sandy, General Bridges' horse, contracted pneumonia. Bridges, who had a shy nature, spent time below deck comforting Sandy and the other horses. He talked to them gently and the extraordinary bond he felt was demonstrated by his willingness to go to these lengths to ensure that the horses were well looked after.

4

Training in Egypt: the Remount Depots

'One day I saw a horse chuck both saddle and bridle'

On arrival in Alexandria, Egypt, in December 1914, many horses were in a terrible condition. Unloading them from the ship involved lifting each one in a sling and hoisting them over the side onto pontoons next to the ships, then towing them to shore. Recovery took at least a month with gentle exercise, grooming and pace training. Moonlit night rides to the pyramids, horse races and carnivals were organised to condition the horses and help form bonds. The soldiers with their new horses, and those who had brought their own, developed and strengthened special bonds as they spent this time together.

Problems developed in the new environment, including a fear of camels, and many horses bolted. Other horses hated the donkeys, so socialising the animals was important. Other problems included the gravelly sand and the wind in the desert environment. Horses' eyes would become red and weeping and the flies would infect them. To combat this problem, lace-like leather headdresses were attached to the head strap of bridles to stop the flies but still allow the horses' good vision. They were called fly-fringes.

Horse wearing a fly fringe in the desert.

The army saddles had narrow bars which would rub the horses' backs — they were very different to the saddles back in Australia, which were broad and cushioned underneath. In Egypt, the constant riding could cause saddle sores which became infected with maggots. To solve the problem, the troopers used

A horse being unloaded at the other end of the journey.

Picture: Australian War Memorial

Rawleigh's Ointment (suitable for man or beast!) combined with thick surplus army blankets from the hospital in Cairo used as saddle blankets.

As well as the difficult physical conditions, the volunteers endured four months of boredom from inaction, and found creative ways to combat this, including races and competitions. Horses had to be conditioned and trained to work in troop formation, to lead and to accept tethering. There were endless drills, shooting dummy targets, and friendly equestrian competitions which included sprint races, flag races and horsemanship tests. Lieutenant Guy Haydon won many events on his mare, 'Midnight'.

There were a surprising number of mascots at camp which included roosters, monkeys, dogs and kangaroos to boost morale—these were given to Cairo Zoo when the soldiers were sent to . Visits to Cairo gave relief to the soldiers, but the Aussie volunteers' disrespect for authority was always evident, directed at the British officers in particular: "We are getting in hot water about not saluting officers in the street," Ion Idriess wrote. "A man would need an automatic arm."

The Light Horse Brigades were sent to fight the Turkish on the Gallipoli Peninsula in May 1915. Of the 6100 horses sent to Gallipoli, very few were put ashore as the terrain was clearly unsuitable, and the regiments served in a dismounted role. Lieutenant-General Sir William Birdwood, in charge of the Gallipoli Campaign, sent the horses back to Egypt. Only some packhorses, mules and speedy horses were needed on the peninsula. It was quickly understood that a dispatch rider service between Headquarters at Suvla Bay and Headquarters at Anzac Cove was needed urgently. The fast horses were used to send urgent messages and to deliver mail. One horse, 'Bill the Bastard' (more of whom later), proved invaluable as a packhorse because of his bulk, strength and endurance. In one instance he carried an urgent message, making the seven-kilometre dash from Suvla Bay to the British Headquarters based at Anzac Cove. Captain Bickworth rode him but was bucked off. The diggers nervously watched as Bill the Bastard was fired at by the Turks. Bill delivered the mail riderless but with a bullet lodged in his flank.

Artwork: John Cox

Training in Egypt: the Remount Depots

Major-General William Bridges is half hidden behind his horse Sandy in this picture taken at Mena camp in Egypt in early 1915.

This life-size bronze statue to commemorate General Bridges' horse Sandy was unveiled in his home town of Tallangatta on 20 May 2023.

Picture: *The Age*

The Australian commander of the First Division, Major-General William Bridges, a tall, reserved man, questioned some of the strategies used at Gallipoli. Unfortunately, he was hit by a sniper's bullet on May 15. Before he died, he requested that his beloved horse, Sandy, be sent back to Australia. Sandy was kept in the care of an Australian Army Vet Corps officer, Captain Leslie Whitfeld, in Egypt before he was transported to France, then in 1918 to the remount depot in England until he was sent home. Sandy was the only Australian horse to be sent home.

Gallipoli

Gallipoli was proving to be disastrous, with the death toll rising dramatically. The ANZACS were unable to take the Turkish trenches high up the cliffs on the ridges. The Light Horsemen from the various regiments who had been sent as reinforcements in May, fought bravely. No doubt they missed the companionship of their horses and riding them in the desert. Instead, they found themselves fighting in trenches as infantry.

On May 16, a further 2250 men and 106 officers from the 2nd and 10th Light Horse regiments were sent to help at Gallipoli. The 8th regiment from Victoria and the 10th from Western Australia were ordered to take control of the Nek.

Saturday 7 August 1915 will forever be cemented in Light Horse memory. This was the day of a brave but tragic assault by the dismounted 3rd Light Horse at the Nek.

The episode is described by the Australian Government as follows: "Naval gunfire and shore-based artillery shelled the Ottoman positions. The bombardment was intended to provide cover for the Australians during the attack. Unfortunately, the barrage ended seven minutes too early, but the officers in charge did not adapt their plans. They held back their men until the appointed time for the charge.

"The delay gave the Turks enough time to set up their machine guns. They were ready for the assault.

"The plan was for the New Zealanders to move down from Chunuk Bair and attack when the Light Horse did. But the New Zealanders had not taken Chunuk Bair as intended, so their support did not come."[1]

Major-General Alexander John Godley, his subordinate Brigadier-General Frederick Hughes and hands-on leader Lt-General John Macquarie 'Bull' Anthill ordered the attack. The ANZACS had to cross open ground and "face a wall of Turkish machine guns that had never left their defending position and were waiting for them", wrote Jonathan King in *Gallipoli Diaries*.

---

1 Department of Veterans' Affairs (2022), Battle of the Nek 7 August 1915, DVA Anzac Portal, www.anzacportal.dva.gov.au/wars-and-missions/ww1/where-australians-served/gallipoli/august-offensive/the-nek

Charles Bean said it was like asking men to run from the back line at one end of a tennis court towards the back line at the other end which was lined with Turks shoulder to shoulder with machine guns blazing.

- 4.30pm: 150 men of the first wave of the 8th Light Horse regiment jumped out of the trenches and were mown down within 30 seconds

- 4.32pm: 150 men of the second wave of the 8th Light Horse regiment met the same fate.

- Lt-Colonel Noel Brazier, who was directly in charge, pleaded with Anthill to stop the slaughter, to no avail.

- 4.45pm: The third wave from the 10th Light Horse regiment was also mown down. One trooper was Wilfred Harper who was seen sprinting towards the enemy like an Olympian. Harper's run was part of the inspiration for Peter Weir's 1981 film *Gallipoli*.

The full horror of this experience was recounted later by Sergeant Evan 'Enie' Bain (10th Regiment). He was in the fourth line, waiting for orders. He had just witnessed the third line from the 10th Light Horse being decimated – His brother died in that line.

"We were just ordinary boys and the war was just a bit of excitement," he wrote. "We were all worried that it would be over before we got there… then over they went… two or three got

EVAN BAIN

Evan 'Enie' Bain was a tall, blue-eyed Scot who arrived in Western Australia with his family when he was 9. His brother Duncan was killed in the line ahead of his at Gallipoli – "I buried him on the beach and had a cross erected to his memory," Bain, known to most as 'Enie', later wrote.

Bain was proud of the war service of himself, his brother Donald and his late brother Duncan. Up until the year before he died in 1982 at the age of 89, he rode in the annual Anzac Day Parade in Perth as a 10th Light Horseman on his groomed horse, in full dress uniform with the emu feather on his slouch hat flying.[3]

---
3 EMIC Social Work: A Story of Practice, Frances Roberta Crawford, 1994, University of Illinois at Urbana-Champaign, US.

CLIFF ST PINNOCK

Charles Clifford Denham St Pinnock, a 27-year-old broker, enlisted at Broadmeadows training camp in Melbourne.

He was badly injured at the Nek, patched up, and two months later sent back to the front.
Pinnock died in August 1916 following shell injuries which required him to have both legs amputated.
He was buried in Rue du Bois Military Cemetery in France.

far enough to get into the trenches. The rest were just scattered out there. Some wounded, some dead. Like if you had cut down a lot of sheaves and they were laying on the ground.

"While the Turks kept firing, we were throwing anything, ropes and puttees, anything at all out to the wounded to catch hold of. Dragging them back, then putting them on stretchers to be taken away.

"Don't tell me that fellas were brave and itching to get out [of the trenches]. No. No. No. No-one was itching to get out. It was too drastic right alongside you…We never questioned. We just accepted it. It was part of the job."[2]

The 8th regiment was decimated in the first two waves. Then the poor men in the 10th, having witnessed the carnage, went over the top to the same fate. The order to stop finally filtered through, but was not heard by all the regiment, so many from the 10th were shot down in the fourth wave. The sound of the onslaught was described by Charles Bean: "…it rose from a fierce cackle into a roar in which you could distinguish neither rifle nor machine gun, but just one continuous roaring tempest. One could not help an involuntary shiver—God help anyone that was out in that tornado. But one knew very well that men were out in it."

Sergeant Cliff St Pinnock, (8th Light Horse, Victoria) who miraculously survived the first wave, said in a letter a week later that he "cried like a child" when roll call was made after the tragedy, as so few men answered. In three quarters of an hour, a total of 234 Light Horsemen were killed and 138 wounded.

2 Evan 'Enie' Bain, *The Ways of Life*, 1977, Elder Smith, UK.

The charge at the Nek was disastrous. The Victorian 8th Light Horse regiment lost 234 men, the WA 10th Light Horse, 83. These figures highlight the ferocity of the attack and the terrible death toll inflicted on men charging with a rifle fixed with a bayonet against the rapid fire of machine guns. It would have been target practice for the Turks. No one could doubt the bravery of the young ANZAC horsemen, who, while conquering fear and obeying orders, knew what fate awaited them. C.E. Bean, in his book *The Story of the Anzac*, said of this event, "for sheer bravery, devoted loyalty and that self-discipline which seldom failed in Australian soldiers, they stand alone in the annals of their country."

Over 300 men were killed in an area the size of about three tennis courts…a tragic episode in this war, and one of pointless slaughter.

Egypt

Back in Egypt, unaware of the carnage, humour was prevalent as new Australian and New Zealand recruits prepared to leave the training grounds for their chance at 'adventure'. Ion Idriess in *The Desert Column* commented on the banter that went on between the 'Aussies' and 'En Zeds', (New Zealanders) as they boarded ships bound for Gallipoli on August 27, 1915, undaunted by the task ahead. "As the En Zeds howled their hair-raising Maori War Song…the Australians were imitating the bleatings of a mob of sheep being yarded, made more realistic by the barkings of men who, of a certainty, had worked in many a station muster."

The decision to commit the AIF, including the Light Horse, to the Gallipoli campaign led to the creation of the First Remount Unit to buy and train horses. It was set up in September 1915 in Egypt and consisted of four squadrons. A second unit was soon established to cope with the need for horses. A quarter of the Light Horse troops were left in Egypt to look after the horses, but it became evident that more men were needed. Older men, including blacksmiths and saddlers, were recruited as grooms to maintain the horses' health. They were affectionately called 'Methusaliers' and 'Horse dung Hussars' because of their age. Other men with specific knowledge of horses and forty rough-riders per squadron were also recruited because the work was hard and dangerous. They had to work with some half-broken and 'outlaw' horses sent from Australia. Lieutenant Banjo Paterson was appointed head of the 2nd Remount Unit which was established at Maadi in December 1915. His unit consisted of thirty-one officers, three veterinary officers, one medical officer and 816 men who included rough-riders, saddlers, blacksmiths, farriers and horse handlers.

Guy Haydon on his beloved Midnight at Holsworthy army base in 1915.

In December 1915, as men returned from Gallipoli, they were reunited with their horses. One soldier, Lieutenant Guy Haydon, looked for his beloved black mare Midnight, but she had been allocated to another regiment. He would not rest until he had arranged a swap to be with his horse. Such was the bond that was formed between a man and his horse.

Gallipoli had been a disaster and the British had failed to control the Turkish forces. The death toll on both sides was horrific. Thirty thousand men were evacuated from the peninsula and the Light Horsemen returned to Egypt. With the return of the men, the original purpose for the Remounts no longer existed, so numbers dropped to two squadrons. The older men went home.

After Gallipoli, the AIF was reorganised into five infantry divisions with 10,000 to 20,000 in each division. They were to be reassigned to the Western Front where the trench warfare was at a stalemate with heavy casualties being endured. The horses there suffered terribly. There were four brigades of Light Horse. Many Light Horsemen were killed so Paterson had to allocate men to horses, adding to the trauma from Gallipoli for the survivors as horses had to be reassigned and new bonds formed.

A major push was planned to drive the Turkish forces out of Palestine as they threatened the security of the Suez Canal. This task was assigned to the Light Horse and thousands of horses were needed for this to happen. Training horses for the trauma of battle included rigid toughening-up drills, making them respond to specific commands and calls, but the hardest job was to train them to stand still as gunshot flew close to their eyes and heads. This training and the humane treatment of the Australian Waler horse were crucial to success in the Middle East. The extraordinary bond between soldier and horse was admired by those who encountered the Australian Light Horse.

Champion rough-rider Sgt Jack Dempsey (2nd Remount Unit) riding a buckjumper at Maadi, Egypt. He had been a horse-breaker in his home town of Leeton, NSW.

In April 1916 the 2nd Remount Unit was relocated for fifteen months to Heliopolis, where a showground and a racecourse were allocated for training. Captain Herbert A. Reid was in charge of Squadron 1 and Banjo Paterson of Squadron 2.

Throughout 1916 the rough-riders worked at full stretch. 12,770 horses and mules were killed, wounded or debilitated on the Western Front and in skirmishes and attacks in the desert. To replace them, the Unit received over 12,200 further animals and issued 11,778 to soldiers during the year. Half of the men at the Unit were rough-riders who were necessary to deal with the unruly horses that were let in. The men suffered many injuries, and in some cases were killed, in the course of their work with the spirited and often aggressive horses.

(From collection of E.O. Green, 2nd Remount Unit)

JACK DEMPSEY

John (Jack) Albert Dempsey was a horse breaker from Leeton, NSW. In the war he directed the work of the rough-riders under the command of Major Banjo Paterson, who described him as "a six-foot-two Australian, straight as a stringy-bark sapling and equally as tough…"

As a young man Dempsey was an excellent athlete, and also put on exhibition buckjumping shows. After the war he returned to work with horses, eventually starting his own livery stable and store. He and Paterson remained life-long friends. Dempsey died in 1950.

According to Paterson, "The racecourse and showgrounds were under a dust cloud all day—15 to 20 riders at a time worked their mounts. Many of them rode a dozen horses a day in addition to their ordinary stable duties." Horses had to be broken in, subdued, conditioned and trained. Draught horses and mules had to be broken to harness. All this was necessary for a mobile assault. Paterson had high regard for these rough-riders, as he commented in *Happy Dispatches*: "Australian rough-riders are the best in the world."

Rough-riders

Rough-riders were the men who trained the horses that bucked (buck-jumpers). One famous rough-rider was Jack Dempsey who was born in the Upper Murray. His father was a horse breaker. Dempsey was 188cm tall, and tough. He made a living by riding outlaw horses in shows. One horse that he rode was a big bay called 'The Rebel' who was said to be the worst buckjumper in Australia. Dempsey took part in a notorious buckjumping contest in Maadi which he won. Some of the witnesses took photos, and years later one was displayed in which, reported the Narrandera Argus, "The horse was standing almost upright on hind legs—for it was in this attitude the horse displayed rare cunning to dislodge the rider…" Dempsey stayed on.

The rough-riders had rough, basic uniforms and specially made saddles. According to Banjo Paterson, the field service uniform for a rough-rider consisted of a shirt and riding breeches, no leggings or puttees, and their socks were pulled up outside the ends of their breeches. They wore elastic-sided boots. They used stock saddles with large knee and thigh pads and a simple ring-snaffle bit that was used back home in the bush.

At the height of training at Heliopolis, Paterson

wrote a letter, dated 26 March 1917, in which he said, "At the present moment I have two men with broken legs, one with a fractured shoulder blade, two with badly crushed ankles and about seven others more or less disabled in hospital at one time out of about 100 riders."

To help keep men and horses fit, race meetings were organised. Also, the Khedivial Sporting Club had race meetings on Saturdays outside Cairo. This was a prestigious club founded in 1882 which attracted officers and wealthy patrons. 'Babanooka', the horse of Colonel Thomas Todd from the 10th Light Horse Regiment, proved himself the best handicap horse in Egypt.

During this training period an intense rivalry developed between the British and Australian cavalry about who had the best horses. The British assumed superiority with their thoroughbreds. To settle the argument, a special day of competition was arranged between the two armies. Guy Haydon (12th Light Horse Regiment) and his horse Midnight were chosen to represent Australia in a three-event contest dubbed the 'Desert Olympics'. Little did the English know that Midnight was, in fact, a well-bred top performance horse, the fastest horse back in the Hunter Valley, NSW.

Guy Haydon, 1916

Haydon was only able to take him to war because the family believed that she would keep him safe due to her courage, speed and sure footedness. (This would prove to be prophetic at Beersheba.)

The first event was a sprint race of a quarter of a mile (400 metres). Midnight won. The second was the 'utility

(Image 1890) State Library of NSW

BANJO PATERSON

During World War I, Andrew Barton (Banjo) Paterson sailed to Europe hoping for an appointment as a war correspondent. Instead, he was attached as an ambulance driver to the Australian Voluntary Hospital in France and later was commissioned as Major to the 2nd Remount Unit of the AIF.

The Remount broke in thousands of horses and mules, shod them, fed them, groomed them, raced them, and trained them for battle conditions.

After the war Paterson returned to journalism and later concentrated on writing. He was a national celebrity until his death in 1941.

Rough-riders in Egypt featured in the photo album of trooper Jack McGrath. Top: Trooper Roy Stanbridge of Queensland; bottom: an unidentified rough rider from South Australia.

Pictures: State Library of Queensand

Trooper Edward (Ned) Kelly, 2nd Remount Unit, tackles a buckjumper, c1916.

Trooper Norman Richards, 2nd Remount, hangs on for grim death.

Corporal Daniel O'Keeffe, 1st Remount Unit, looking a bit unstable.

A trooper identified as Charles Dowdels is flung off while training at Heliopolis racecourse.

flags' event involving obstacles and using swords, completing tasks against the clock. Midnight won. The third was an equitation (horsemanship) test involving dressage and, to, everyone's amazement, Midnight won.

The Australians had won the Cavalry Desert Olympics, though this was not reported back to England. It did, however, signal the beginning of a cultural shift in the respect the British Calvary had for the Australians, and as the desert campaigns evolved they acknowledged the tougher bush-reared Australian horses had come into their own. In fact, they rated the Walers to be some of the finest cavalry horses ever seen.[5]

> **One reason why rough-riders had work to do**
>
> One big stock supplier from Queensland had just shipped 600 broken-in horses when the Army sent a rush order for 100 more.
>
> The supplier did not have the extra 100 broken in, so he sent 100 unbroken horses which had what they called the 'barcoo polish on them'.
>
> This meant that the horses had been forced into a race (long narrow pen) in the yards, and riders had been able to bridle and ride the entire 100 horses a few yards along the race in two days. Thus the supplier could swear that every horse had been ridden.

Rough-rider displays, with the backdrop of the Nile and the pyramids, became famous. People such as Egyptian notables, English celebrities, aristocratic ladies and the British Commander in Chief, Archibald Murray, sat through whole shows. At these shows some dangerous feats eventuated. Banjo Paterson described some incidents: "A big chestnut threw himself straight over backwards and narrowly missed pinning his rider to the ground; A waspish bay mare refused to move at all when mounted, and crouched right down till her chest nearly touched the ground." ... the rider kicked, and "as he did so, she unleashed a terrible spring, shot him out of the saddle and sent him soaring in the air..."

Some horses bolted off into the desert. But despite the tough conditions, broken bones and bruised egos, humour was evident among the rough-riders. Slippery army saddles were dubbed 'patent self-emptiers' by some, and jokes were made about each others' riding abilities. Paterson commented that they

---

5 *Midnight Warhorse*, compiled by Peter Haydon, Bloomfield, p35

were "possibly the best lot of men that ever were got together to deal with rough horses."

Banjo Paterson's role in this training camp in Egypt was crucial. The army needed fit, trained horses for the Desert Campaign, 1916-1918. The Australian horses were ideal because by and large they had good background/breeding, were about 14 to 16 hands, were thickset and weighed on average 500kg. They had been acclimatised for a year and had adjusted to their diet and the sandy conditions. They also set a good pace as fast walkers and could last longer than the British horses, as thoroughbreds often trotted and tired sooner. Most importantly, they were well cared for and loved. Paterson spent four years buying, requisitioning and preparing suitable horses for the army; animals that had to face extreme conditions and remain calm in the face of danger. The best horses had to be assigned to soldiers first, even when those in command wanted to choose the very best for themselves.

Paterson wrote about the endearing qualities of horses in many of his poems. His pseudonym 'Banjo' came from a horse—it was the name of his favourite family horse, and he used it as the pseudonym under which he wrote some of his early works in *The Bulletin* magazine. Paterson knew how to get the best from horses and was well respected by the men who worked with him. He was, however, regarded as a 'wild colonial boy' by the English aristocracy and the Australian Waler horse was overlooked in comparison to the well-bred thoroughbreds used by the British Cavalry. General Edmund Allenby commented to Paterson when in Palestine, "Your Australian horses are a common, hairy-legged lot." He changed his assessment of the magnificent horses later in the campaign.

The third Remount training camp was based at Moascar, near Ismaelia, Egypt, from July 1917 until the end of the war in 1918. It was the largest and most important depot west of the Suez. As with the previous depot, Paterson put on big shows to make the remount depot celebrated. He advertised buckjumping show riders and horse breakers, and 'Bill the Bastard' was billed as the "unrideable one". The 'Moascar Sports' were held, testing strength and skill. There were buckjumping exhibitions, obstacle races in which the riders had to gallop over hurdles, dismount, fire, and gallop home; the rescue race in which a trooper rode his horse, picked up a comrade, jumped over obstacles and returned. Also included were the relay race, half-mile championship, sack race, tent pegging and tug of war. These games were excellent for morale and skill development.

In all, over 50,000 horses for battle and 10,000 horses and mules for carrying supplies went through the training 1000 at a time, and all had to be fed, exercised and groomed. Paterson was in awe of the Light Horsemen. The "majority of Light Horsemen are good riders, they understand other riders, understand horses, know how to treat them, as well as how to ride them", he said.

The work done by the remount units and in particular, the horses, was often overlooked in British and Australian war reports, yet this training was vital to military success. From Magdhaba in 1917, the Desert Column advanced fifty kilometres to El Arish, made a night march of another thirty kilometres to a Turkish outpost, overcame it in a fierce skirmish and then rode back to El Arish, all in less than forty hours. At Rafa, the first battle of Gaza and at Beersheba, the units were persistent and mobile. The march on Jerusalem and raids east of the Jordan saw the remounts endure difficult terrain and horrific conditions. Finally, in September 1918, they covered nearly 1000 kilometres in thirty-eight days. This was called 'the Great March', which ended at Damascus.

The ability to have fit and trained animals to replace those killed, wounded or broken down by the workload was an amazing effort and is testament to the training provided at the Remount Depots by the rough-riders and to the Waler horses themselves.

Picture by permission

Photograph shows Lieutenant George Simpson Millar on his horse 'The Outlaw', which he describes as an "ex Remounts cast off."

Lt Millar (1892-1973) served with the 5th Light Horse Regiment. He appeared in several photos with The Outlaw.

Sheer joy — Men of then 6th Light Horse toss one of their number in a blanket prior to the departure for home of the 'first joiners' — those who had joined in 1914.

5

Conditions on the Western Front, 1915–1918.

*'Horses would spook at screams of pain and if there was shelling,
the frightened horses would jolt as they shied in fear.'*

From the beginning in 1914, on the Western Front in Belgium, the English cavalry was used as a shield for the soldiers. The cavalry would charge, then dismount and fight with the infantry in the trenches. Horse losses were high. The horses were important also for transport, where there were many dangers along the roads. Horses in harness travelled long distances under stress, often being shot at and shelled.

In December 1915, the Light Horse, after being reunited with their horses after the tragedy at Gallipoli, were reorganised to allow two regiments to be broken up to form a reconnaissance squadron in France. The 13th Light Horse consisted of three squadrons (400) men and part of the fourth regiment—two squadrons (256) men. They were moved to the Western Front in France between March and June 1916. They were issued with steel helmets and gas masks for the men and horses. The 13th, known as "the Devil's Own," has often been overlooked in official war records.

Conditions in Europe during 1916 were appalling. The horses went straight from the dry climate in Egypt to France's worst winter in thirty years. The mud was so deep in some areas where shells had exploded that man and horse could drown. The horses were no match for machine guns, barbed wire and trenches. German machine guns cut a swathe through the horses brought into the assault at the Somme. In one day, 20,000 British soldiers died and many horses died from exhaustion, exposure to the weather, disease and machinegun-fire. The horses had to drag carts carrying the wounded but often got stuck in the mud and had to be put down. Many became nervous due to the constant shelling and the deadly gas released into the trenches affected the horses as well.

The winter of 1917 was as treacherous as that of 1916 had been. The Battle of Passchendale was the most costly for horses. The 13th and part of the 4th Light Horse were sent to this battlefield. The mules and horses suffered from shelling, rain, deep holes in the field and sinking in the mud. Some horses had to pull heavy artillery, carry supplies and draw the field ambulances. The machine gunners of the 4th Light Horse Regiment had to have a heavy gun strapped to one horse and the magazine and ammunition strapped to another horse behind as both were led into battle. Attached to the Infantry was a unit called the Horse Retrieval Unit; horse and cart had to retrieve the wounded. They often got bogged, and horses shied at the shelling.

A Light Horse mule team transporting supplies to forward positions in the Ypres sector in Belgium is stuck in the mud. 19 October 1917

The horse-drawn field ambulances had a terrible time keeping up with the number of casualties. These horses were often in poor condition and could be found standing in the far corners of their makeshift paddocks trembling in fear. They were badly affected by strain, the cold and often hunger. The constant bombardments affected them, just as it did the soldiers. Barry Heard, in his novel, *Tag*, wrote that, "Many horses were shell-shocked and not willing to face the battlefield…The solution was to encourage and reassure them, not whip them into submission."

One of the big problems was carts getting bogged in the mud while trying to bring back the wounded from the battlefield. The Australians came up with a solution, which was to make a bush sled like the ones they used back home for carting fence posts, where they used a corrugated sheet of iron. On the Western Front, they improvised by using the fork of a tree as a sled, the frame being about 4 ft. wide by 8 ft. long, and putting a rough timber platform on top large enough to carry six men. One horse could drag this contraption over the mud. Another solution was to empty the cart on the field, unhitch the horses and lead them back to firmer ground, have a long rope attached and pull the cart to the road using men and horses.

Gas was the hardest weapon to endure. Often delivered by screaming artillery shells, it burnt the eyes and throat and created intense pain in the lungs. The horses hated wearing gas masks and once they knew the routine to put them on, they resisted. To overcome this, the routine was changed. Instead of trying to put the mask on immediately before moving to the battlefield, the soldiers would put the mask on randomly after feeding, during the night or while the horse was being brushed. This was an example of how training methods required gentle coercion and infinite patience.

British picture shows the gas masks used for horses on the Belgian front.

Field ambulance

The field ambulances had incredibly difficult times. The horse-drawn carts had four wheels and a canvas top. They were pulled by two horses and two men were on the cart. Each cart could hold twelve wounded: eight sitting and four lying down. There were always too many wounded and the decision had to be made who to take and who to leave. The horses sensed the madness and stress as they headed out to get casualties and this could lead to their behaving erratically. The men would have to encourage the edgy animals out towards the battlefield where they would sense death and suffering, and often they were whipped and slapped viciously with the long reins, cursed and yelled at to get them to carry on. On the battlefield the horses would sometimes spook at screams of pain and cries for help, and if there was shelling, frightened horses would shy in fear.

There were horse handlers to help, however, and their main message was to treat the horses carefully. "Don't flog them to get them moving," they would instruct. "Gain their confidence, talk to them and build up their trust." Each platoon had sixty horses, two per man. If the men made the horses their own stalls and spent time in watering, feeding and brushing them, giving them names—and some famous ones were Bonkeye, Dribbles, Sulky Sam and Wrinkle Bum—a bond grew. At least one hour a day was

An Australian horse-drawn ambulance moves down a muddy track taking wounded men to a casualty clearing station. To the left a transport wagon moves up to the forward area with supplies. 28 August 1916, Pozieres area, France.

needed with the horses. "Halter and lead them for a walk away from the horror, then brush for 20 minutes. Then lead them to the feed trough and make sure they get a decent feed and stand there with them. Scratch them and ruffle their ears," was one instruction. If this was done, the soldier would have "a mate and the horse would do what was asked of it."

By March 14 1917, the Germans had been forced back and the surrounding country was open so the Light Horse were needed to patrol, checking on the enemy's whereabouts. Lance-Corporal Geoff Gilbert recalled the experience many years later (as quoted in *My Corps Cavalry* by Doug Hunter). "Out in front...riding over at the walk to draw enemy fire—rotten shots the Fritz must have been for any of us to survive. We were to ride over the rise to where we would be in full view of the enemy between Bertincourt and Vulu Wood and draw fire...then gallop back."

At the battle of Arras in France during April and May 1917, the Australian Light Horse proved their worth. The German army had strong, fixed defences, so to plan an attack, the 1st Anzac needed detailed information about these defences. Gathering this information was the duty of the 13th Light Horse regiment. Communication between the brigade and battalion headquarters was by 'gallopers'. Gallopers were the Light Horsemen who had to hold their nerve as each horse chose its footing carefully on the uneven ground, avoiding muddy shell holes or barbed wire. Two troopers, Frank Barry, a 21-year-old Irish waiter who enlisted in Melbourne, and Henry 'Fen' Pillow, 21, from Geelong, were awarded military medals for their duties on this task carried out under heavy shell-fire and in full view of the enemy. It was noted by one witness that in preparing for the mission, "Frank Barry felt his horse press closer and nuzzle his arm. 'Ginger' was no stranger to the roar of artillery and the zip of machine-gun bullets…He stroked the horse's neck. 'Easy Ginger,' he said."

Later in September 1917, a low ridge running through the eastern edge of Polygon Wood near Ypres in Flanders was attacked and taken by the Australians by midday. Mounted patrols of the 13th Light Horse had patrolled during the day. They also had to patrol the main traffic route on the Menin Road in the Passchendale-Zonnebeek sector. The patrols were often carried out under heavy enemy shelling.

The German army withdrew to the Hindenberg Line and Lt-General (later Sir) John Monash of Australia sent the 13th ahead of the Australian Corps to retain contact with the enemy. The 13th was told to go hard against machinegun fire. General Monash said of the Light Horse, "These troops more than justified their employment by bold, forward reconnaissance and energetic pressure on enemy rear guards."[6]

Major T. Williams of the 4th Light horse was awarded a DSO for his work and that of his squadron. To quote his citation, "This officer with his squadron was continuously on duty. The manner in which he worked his patrols to harass the enemy and gain information showed excellent daring leadership.'

By 1918 the Germans were retreating, so small Light Horse patrols went forward to locate machinegun posts left by the Germans to delay the Allied advance. These patrols would spread, swing out wide to each flank, then move in on guns positioned from both sides at once in a pincer movement. They would then scatter for shelter. On 24 April, a troop of the 13th Light Horse were placed under the command of Lt-Colonel Charles Watson. They combed and probed the battlefield for information and quickly located enemy gun positions. On the morning of 25 April, four Light Horsemen rode into the village of Villers-Bretoneux under spasmodic machinegun fire. The men dismounted and

---

6 John Monash, *The Australian Victories in France in 1918*. First published 1920

leaving one man with the horses, rushed the machinegun post, capturing four prisoners. Corporal Frank Lanagan, a farmer from Rupanyup in Victoria, then went forward on foot alone and returned with another prisoner and information. The patrol remounted and returned to their headquarters with the information and the prisoners. Lanagan was awarded the Distinguished Conduct Medal for his actions on 24 and 25 April. This account of the action is based on his citation.

Brigade Headquarters continued to use the Light Horse for the rest of that day in April to keep tabs on enemy movements as well as assessing the morale of their own troops on the battlefield. Villers-Bretonneux was captured in part due to the intelligence gathered by the small band of horsemen who crossed and recrossed the inhospitable battlefield.

Another successful action took place across the Somme towards the town of Peronne. In darkness, before dawn on 30 August 1918, a troop of the 13th Light Horse was sent to establish a base at Fargny Wood. Patrols were sent north-east and east to report on enemy movement. A steady stream of information was sent to headquarters using a succession of riders. Traralgon-born Sergeant Gordon Drane, patrol commander, received a military medal for his work that day.

The despatch rider

This vivid account describes an individual action by Frank Barry to deliver a message.

"The rider swung into the saddle, urging the horse from the disused gun-pit, and headed into the man-made storm where every yard threatened wounds or death for man and beast. This was the first of many despatches Frank Barry and Ginger would carry."

Success on the Western Front in 1918 can certainly be attributed to the genius of John Monash and the bravery of the soldiers, and Monash rightly acknowledges the role of the Light Horse, too.

"They shone in triumphant Australian offensives of Amiens, Albert and Hindenburg Lines," Monash wrote. "They were the horsemen who had ventured to draw the machine-gunners' fire; theirs were the resolute patrols that guarded open flanks and manned traffic posts on shell-riven roads; they were the riders who went undaunted through the storm to deliver the messages." He called them, 'My Corps Cavalry'. They were the 'eyes' of the armies. The 13th corps cavalry provided information, communications, liaison and protection to the commanders by mounted patrolling. Their versatility made them invaluable as despatch riders, scouts, flank guards, escorts and screens. The danger was unrelenting. Despatch riders and horses had to cover hundreds of yards of open ground swept by shell and bullet. "The rider must hold his nerve; a horse had to be allowed to choose its footing in the broken ground. A racing horse soon became terrified and a terrified horse would soon be down a muddy shell hole or tangled in wire," a commentator later wrote.[7]

The Western Front was disastrous on many levels. There were many horse casualties and it was crucial to keep them fit and healthy. Horse deaths during battles resulted from shell shock, falls in shell holes, drowning in mud, starvation, poison gas and wounds from shells and bombs. Foot injuries were caused by mud, shrapnel wounds and cruel four-pointed metal objects called caltrops designed to disable horses and which would push into the sole of the hoof, right up to the joint, pushing up dirt, which would cause infections. Other deaths were due to disease including equine influenza, ringworm, sand colic, a hoof disease known as seedy toe, septic sores, strangles (respiratory disease), exhaustion and exposure.

The horses served many purposes in the war. Initially they were used as cavalry mounts, but with the development of trench warfare, barbed wire, the tank and machine guns, they were needed for other tasks. They pulled ambulances, carried supplies and pulled field guns, where six were needed for each gun. In the Middle East, they had to travel sometimes up to sixty hours without water, the conditions they had to work under including heat, sand, sniper attack and fatigue. In Europe, horses suffered a high death rate from machinegun fire, harsh winters, mud and constant artillery bombardment. They faced the same traumas the soldiers had to face. The bond between man and horse was severely tested.

The Light Horse on the Western Front were disbanded. The horses were auctioned off to Frenchmen to use on their farms. These horses were stockhorse and part-racehorse, not what the French farmers were used to. There were accounts of locals careering through the towns of northern France clinging to the backs of animals whose breeding was better than they were accustomed to. Incidents of carts out of control and ploughs bouncing across fields were noted.

---

[7] www.lancers.org.au/site/Light_Horse_France.php, prepared by John Howells, 2007

6

The Light Horse in the Middle East

'Long rides, fatigue, sleepless nights, in a grim wilderness, one of the harshest regions in the world.'

The Light Horse faced a very different challenge from the infantry in France and Flanders. They had a better chance of surviving than did their compatriots. They did not have to wait in trenches with bayonets fixed, listening for the artillery barrage to stop and for an officer to send them into no man's land to face German machinegun fire. Accordingly, the casualty list sustained in three years in the Middle East was often exceeded in as many days by the 'poor bloody infantry' on the Western Front.

While many Light Horsemen suffered on the Western Front and little progress was made amidst a horrific death toll, the Light Horse would be forever remembered for its crucial role in bringing about the end of the war in the Palestine/Syria Campaign. This was a sustained, active cavalry push on a huge scale—desert warfare where success depended on horses. Many of the horses and mules used over the three-year campaign were under the control of A.B. Paterson and the Remount Unit that he ran so well. This extraordinary role needs to be highlighted because, without the horses, such success would not have been achieved. The British needed to keep Egypt as it was strategically important: the Suez Canal linked the Red Sea and the Mediterranean. Palestine had been part of Turkey's empire for hundreds of years and lay on Egypt's north-east border across the Sinai Desert. After the evacuation from Gallipoli in December 1915, the Allies resorted to Plan B: this was to "land in Egypt and advance snake-like along the Sinai Peninsula from the Suez Canal and up through the Holy Land." The commander of this campaign, General Murray, was left with three infantry divisions, the Anzac Mounted Division and yeomanry. The Turkish Army had three divisions, the help of 4000 Bedouins and German aircraft and pilots.

TOGETHER THEY FACED HELL

Sinai, 1916

The Sinai Desert was harsh terrain for the Light Horse.

Corporal Austin Edwards, 1st Light Horse, with his horse Taffy and equipment. Edwards was wounded at Romani; during the battle, Taffy stood still for his wounded rider to remount and escape.

Desert Campaign, Sinai 1916

Major-General Harry Chauvel became Commander of the Anzac Mounted Division which consisted of three brigades of Light Horse and one of New Zealand mounted riflemen. Their task was to keep the Turks from attacking the Suez Canal, so they were ordered to push the Turks from the Sinai.

Everything had to be carried by the horsemen and their horses. The men had canvas haversacks over the shoulders which included extra clothes, food and personal possessions; they had a one-litre water bottle and bandolier, .303 rifle slung over the shoulder, bullets in pouches on the belt, a bayonet and scabbard. The horse would have a special military saddle and across the front a rolled greatcoat and waterproof groundsheet would be tied. A mess tin, canvas water bucket and nosebag with a day's grain would be slung at the back of the saddle. A heel rope and picket line and a leather case with two horse-shoes, a blanket carried in a roll spread under the saddle and a billy and tin would complete the load. The horse would be carrying 130 to 150 kilos fully laden.

There were five distinct theatres of war: 1 The initial fight at Romani, 1916. 2 The transitional period along the Palestine border, the Gaza-Beersheba line, from March to October 1917. 3 Judean Hills—hilltop to hilltop, late 1917 to January 1918. 4 Jordan Valley to Jaffa, 1918. 5 Damascus, 1918.

BATTLE OF ROMANI, 3 to 5 August 1916

This was the first major battle of the campaign. For four months at the start of 1916, the Light Horse endured trying conditions in the Sinai Desert. It was thus by one writer: "Life for both soldiers and horses in the desert was tough…the intolerable blaze of the

Picture: Australian War Memorial

Mounted hide of a Light Horse, kitted up for the desert campaign.

midsummer sun and the stress of moving through burning sand weakened the men."

A lot of time was spent waiting and patrolling. To relieve the tension, there was a bit of larking around. An example of this involved a Queenslander, Freddy Campbell of the 5th Light Horse Regiment, who thought the world of his horse, Doreen. Every now and then he would throw his arms around her neck and give her a hug. Two mates decided to play a trick on Freddy. "About midnight they took old Doreen and put her in another troop. The whistle went to quietly saddle up and stand to. No Doreen. Then he started to bellow, 'stop the bloody war, stop the bloody war, Doreen's gone'. The other troop were about 50 feet away and someone yelled, 'who owns this ruddy thing over here? come and get this horse'. Freddy got the world speed record for getting over there to get Doreen. Laugh, Christ almighty."[8]

The desert was a hellhole, a wasteland of sand and rock and desert winds. The Turks believed they could take Egypt by first capturing Romani, then the Suez Canal, and take control. There were skirmishes and unexpected meetings of Turkish patrols coming from Palestine to test the Light Horse. The heat—40-plus degrees—wind, flies and meagre rations took their toll on the men. The horses, also, somehow had to be kept fit, fed and watered.

In April 1916, the British 5th Yeomanry had scouted ahead. They had a British line of outposts across 35 kilometres to the centre at Romani. They were to warn if the Turks were advancing. On April 22, the 5th was attacked by the Turks. It was a surprise attack. A scout reported that there were survivors and headed back to warn the Army.

On 23 April 1916, Major Shanahan received an urgent message to ride with a squadron of 128 troopers to Oghratina, a village 40km from the Suez Canal in the Sinai Desert to help the British 5th mounted cavalry, who had been attacked by the Turks. 'Bill the Bastard,' ridden by Shanahan, was to lead the column as he was the biggest horse and showed no fear. Bill had been wounded at Gallipoli. Whilst the horse was recovering from his injury in the vet sickbay, Shanahan struck up a friendship with him by talking to him, taking him on daily walks and using the secret weapon, licorice! Bill was assigned to Shanahan on the Desert Campaign.

They headed out one night on a trek into unknown territory. As they went deeper into the desert, they encountered mist and it was freezing. As they were heading up a hill, Bill the Bastard became unsettled and refused to move. When kicked he reared up. Shanahan dismounted to see what was wrong with Bill. He walked to the top of the rise and saw a drop into a ravine. Bill had saved the men from certain death.

After a five-hour march through the desert, they came across wounded members of

8 Story by Trooper Peter Kerr, 5th Light Horse, written by granddaughter Narelle Wynn at www.lighthorse.org.au/trooper-peter-kerr

the British cavalry at dawn. The men had escaped on foot but told of 300 prisoners who were left. The troopers galloped towards the village but were met with a horrific sight. The bodies of over 250 cavalrymen had been dismembered and strewn about the village. It is believed that the Bedouin desecrated the bodies after the Turks had killed them. This unsettled the men and horses. They had never come across such a brutal scene.

A British biplane spotted the Turkish Army moving west into the Sinai towards the British-held town of Romani, which had the biggest oasis in the area and was a strategic site. If they defeated the British they would move to Cairo and claim Egypt. General Chauvel knew that they had to be stopped. The Turks had 25,000 infantry and 20,000 camels. For three months during May, June and July they searched for the Turkish forces. It was summer, with temperatures sometimes reaching towards 50°C. They set out on long, gruelling rides, 60 kilometres a day with 27 hours of unbroken reconnaissance. The desert had high, steep hills and deep, dark valleys. The horses would sink deep into the sand. They had short rations, were short of water, suffered from lack of sleep and stumbled across only meagre wells and palm hods, or oases. Wells were the life-blood of the desert.

The troops would often move by night or get up at 3am while it was cool, to search and hide from German planes in the palm hods. The long night marches took their toll. "…Men and horses were dropping off at the oddest times and in the oddest positions, and many men and horses came down in the dust…Dense clouds of dust almost blinded

2nd Light Horse camp at a palm hod (oasis) in the Sinai desert near Romani, 1916.

the tired horses, which collided with one another in the dark," wrote Lt-Colonel Guy Powles of the NZ Mounted Rifles.

However, despite the conditions of long rides, fatigue and sleepless nights in one of the harshest regions in the world, the Light Horse regiments were up early, were ready for fighting and had instant mobility. In the open desert one mounted regiment could defeat 2000 enemy soldiers. Praise was also given to the horses, one observer noting that, "The horses'… powers of endurance were remarkable…sometimes being without water for 50 hours…they were simply marvellous." During the daytime, the scorching 'khamsin'* winds were fierce and in the extreme heat many men would get sunstroke and tired horses would just flop. Ion Idriess described a typical dawn in the desert:

> "The sun rose, a ball of quivering fire, hurrying from the east, a wind straight from a furnace. The horses bent their heads and gasped…I think this is the most hellish wind I've experienced."

Reconnaissance patrols during the day took their toll. An example of the damage that could be inflicted by the conditions occurred in 1916 when the NZ Canterbury and 6th Regiment went out to scout the area. Each man had only one quart water bottle (four cups of water). Heat stress overcame the men and their horses. Some men were described as raving and stragglers were semi-conscious in their saddles. They came staggering in on open-mouthed horses whose eyes were bulging in their sockets. The 6th had camped in the open desert. Fifty men and three officers went down with sunstroke. Some of the men lay comatose for hours and horses were sick for some time…After that, all men got an extra water bottle and as often as they could they would conduct night marches.

Henry Gullett, official war correspondent, noted the conditions under which they labored: "blistering heat…blinding sandstorms…water scarce, heat oppressive and dust perpetual and suffocating."

Finding water was crucial for survival. The commander of Ion Idriess's 5th Light Horse Regiment, Lieutenant Colonel Lachlan Wilson, out of necessity knocked together a piece of equipment used in Queensland to find water. The ingenious invention was called the spear-point pump. It consisted of a pointed, perforated tube hammered into the sand. It was easy to carry and in a few minutes it could be unpacked and driven into the sand. It could draw water in under a quarter of an hour. By the time the men had laid out the light canvas troughing for their horses, a supply of water was ready to be pumped out. The water was brackish but fit for horses to drink. Prior to this invention it had taken two men half a day to reach water by digging.

* hot dry sandy winds

Care for the horses in the difficult desert conditions was time-consuming but essential. The camps had long picket-lines—rope lines to which the horses were tethered—which were anchored to buried sandbags. Men would take off the saddles, groom and feed the horses, and tend to their ailments. Sometimes they hauled water from the ancient wells. "How the neddies pressed forward to drink," wrote trooper George Auchterlonie later. "There has long been a likeable comradeship between each man and his horse."

William (Bill) Griffiths commented, "a man's horse is his home and his saddle his pillow." He claimed that hunger and thirst were problems but worse was lack of sleep. At times on long marches, he would see his horse 'weeping,' the tears running down its cheeks, from lack of sleep. He would wipe its eyes.

Some horses did not like to be last on a march, so if the rider fell asleep the horse would soon make its way to the front to be leader of the group. Some riders fell asleep and fell off their horses.

Two Australian Light Horsemen feed water to an ailing horse in the Sinai Desert, 1917.

By August, Harry Chauvel, with Major Michael Shanahan and the regiment, formed part of the first line of defence of Romani, which formed a natural defensive position as it sat behind a maze of sand dunes and hills which made approaches difficult for attacking. It was dotted with wells which provided a good source of water. Its long history includes occupation by Egyptian armies going back to Alexander the Great, and Napoleon trod this route in 1801.

The British had decided to take an active offensive role using the 1st Light Horse Brigade—the 1st, 2nd and 3rd Light

Major Michael Shanahan mounted on Bill the Bastard. In one wartime incident, Shanahan was wounded and lost consciousness. Bill was reported to have sensed this and carried him back three kilometres to reach help.

Horse regiments—to push the Turks from Romani. This was to stop the Turkish threat to the Suez Canal. So Chauvel had 1700 Light Horsemen to hold the line against 25,000 Turks. The troops had to endure days of extreme heat and swirling winds. The flies were irritating. Sunburn and blisters were constant companions. Chauvel's plan was to draw the Turks to them, use the horses to charge, then fall back; keep the Turks fighting as their supplies were limited; attack at night, keep them fighting till morning. The Light Horse would have the advantage of water in the wells at Romani and the Turks would have no water. It would already be hot by 6am.

At 11.30pm on the night of 3 August 1916, the Australians had spotted Turks creeping out of the dark night to surprise the troops, but Chauvel had placed the 1st Light Horse across the end of the British line to defend their position. It was a tense night of alertness and waiting, and by 1am on 4 August, the battle for Romani had begun. Ion Idriess wrote that "the Turks seemed to rise out of the very sand in overwhelming numbers".

Painting by Jennifer Marshall depicting 'Galloping Jack' Royston encouraging his troopers in battle.
©Jennifer Marshall

Painting by Jennifer Marshall depicting Bill the Bastard with five men on board.
©Jennifer Marshall

The Light Horse Brigade was greatly outnumbered. Soldiers could hear the Turkish battle-cry, "Allah! Allah! Finish Australia!" Idriess described the battle cry as "a terrible scream".

The Light Horse were positioned around a massive dune known as Mount Royston, named after a charismatic Light Horse officer, Brigadier 'Galloping Jack' Royston.

"Flashes of gunfire from both sides lit up the darkness," Idriess wrote. "Pitch black though it was, these inexperienced Aussies now had to stand and fight or die in bloody hand-to-hand combat."

Heroics were performed that night. The Turks attacked Mount Meredith and Wellington Ridge. Brigadier Royston, commanding the 1st Light Horse, raced back and forth encouraging troops and issuing orders. "Keep your heads down lads, stick to it, stick to it, you are making history today!" He wore out eleven horses that night, encouraging the outnumbered diggers.

General Shanahan, riding Bill the Bastard, arrived at the westernmost outpost and found the bodies of Tasmanian horsemen strewn about. He checked the men and then heard voices from Tasmanian survivors. He turned back to help at full gallop. He found four men on foot. Some Turks rushed at them but Bill charged. Shanahan called to the wounded men to mount the big chestnut. Two got on his back and a man took each stirrup. Bill was carrying five men.

"Under constant enemy fire the big Waler galloped, snorting and sweating, flat out over soft sand for more than a kilometre, carrying his load of five troopers to safety." The worst buckjumper anyone had known did not buck; it was if he knew how vital it was to get the men to safety. At the Australian headquarters in the oasis of Bir et Maler, a kilometre or two from Romani, the troopers dismounted and Bill was checked and watered. Shanahan patted Bill and commented, "You are a marvel, my mate, an absolute bloody marvel." This episode was an amazing effort, and highlights the incredible bond between Shanahan and his horse.

There was little rest for the troops. When the column headed towards Wellington Ridge, they met a Turkish infantry contingent on a nearby ridge. The New Zealanders defended this ridge. Bitter fighting continued through the day in the hot, unforgiving sun. The bond between men and their horses was severely tested. An example of the faithfulness of horses is an account of Corporal Austin Edwards who was seriously wounded at the Battle of Romani. His horse, Taffy, stood still, with the battle raging, and waited for his wounded rider to remount and escape.

GALLOPING JACK ROYSTON

Brigadier-General John Robinson ('Galloping Jack') Royston commanded the 12th Light Horse Regiment in 1916. He temporarily took over the 2nd Light Horse Brigade at Romani during General Ryrie's absence, earning the nickname of Galloping Jack from his Australian troops for galloping around the battlefield with "astounding energy and courage". Royston was born in South Africa and first led Australian troops during the Boer War, and gained a lifetime affinity with and respect for the Australian soldiers he served with.

Taffy and Corporal Austin Edwards, 1916.
(Colourised image*)

*Image source: facebook.com/WalerDB/posts/austin-edwards-taffy-sig-corp-a-w-edwards-1st-light-horse-regt-in-palestine-taff/965237856995871

A light moment: Brigadier-General Royston offers his horse a drink from his mug of tea. Source: *Light Horse* by Elyne Mitchell and Chauvel Collection

Reinforcements did not arrive at Romani until about 2pm. Chauvel ordered the remaining 1st Brigade to help the New Zealanders, then brought in the second and third brigades with British artillery. This fight was essential to halt the Turkish advance. They held on through the night, exhausted. By dawn on August 5, the 500-strong 2nd Light Horse regiment which included the Wellington Rifles (New Zealand), led by Chauvel on his chestnut mare, entered to relieve the exhausted 1st Light Horse who had held a thin line. They had dug themselves into the sand and lay, firing.

Turkish resistance collapsed. The Turks were demoralised and needed water, but got only the brutal sun. They were defeated. This was a major achievement as it meant Turkish hopes of taking control of the Suez were dashed. The combination of Australian and New Zealand mounted troops, the Anzacs, proved to be successful. The Australians nicknamed the Wellington Regiment, which fought as part of the 2nd Light Horse throughout August, "the Well and Trulies". For Light Horseman Ion Idriess, "the En-Zeds are first-class fighting men, and I don't think they grumble as much as we do. They shave oftener, anyway."

Against the odds they had halted the Turkish forces. The battle had been hard-fought and lasted two days and two nights. It was the first decisive victory gained by

Loading camels at a railhead in Palestine 1917.
(Colourised Frank Hurley image)

the British land forces. Chauvel was clever. Turkish forces had outnumbered the Anzacs, so he used heat and thirst to his advantage. It was, Chauvel wrote, "the empty Turkish water bottle that won the battle". Exhausted and battle-weary, the Light Horse moved forward. Many of the horses were wounded and sore, but they had to continue on with their battered riders.

No representatives of the Australian press were sent to cover the campaign in the Sinai. There was a perception that Egypt was the place to be if you did not want to fight: the real fighting was on the Western Front. While Romani was the first great victory, British propaganda downplayed the Australians' role to the point where it appeared the battle was won by Britain with Australians and New Zealanders taking part. Very few Anzacs received awards after the battle. Chauvel himself received no credit. Chauvel commented that the Anzac Mounted Division "put up a performance which is beyond all precedent".

George Auchterlonie was a farmer from Narracan in Victoria. Prior to returning home after the war he completed a year's course in agriculture in Scotland.

Auchterlonie died in 1949. His war diaries were later published by his daughter, Gloria.

When he read Murray's despatch covering the Romani operation his reaction was immediate. "I am afraid my men will be very angry when they see it … I cannot understand why the old man cannot do justice to those to whom he owed so much."

Later, General Murray did praise the Anzac troops, and told the war office that "these Anzac troops are the keystone to the defence of Egypt."

After this decisive Romani battle the Light Horse continued their desert push. There were German Taube plane attacks, snipers and constant skirmishes to contend with. Sometimes the horses would not make much noise if hit. "We'd hear a heavy smack! and know a horse had been hit," wrote Idriess.

"The poor brute mostly got it through the stomach. The horse would nose around among his mates, shake himself, and five minutes later roll on the sand. It was the beginning of the end."

There were many casualties and death lurked in the dunes. Trooper George Auchterlonie, a Victorian farmer in the 8th Light Horse, said, "The horses, which had a very trying time, were able to pull themselves together, tho' their ranks were considerably thinned and it was common to come across groups of [horses] lying dead in a hollow." The troopers had to be prepared to march in the early hours, often at 3am, and continue for several days. The horses would be about done.

"Talk about sleepy men, it was our second night without sleep and all had great trouble to keep their eyes open," Auchterlonie wrote. Supplies of food and water were scarce: "Horses were only getting nearly all crushed peas while we are still on tinned dog and biscuits." This humorous reference to bully beef was common to the Diggers. Conditions were hard for the horses also. "…we finally got the saddles off, had only been off 15 minutes in three days."

The war in the desert consisted of endless night marches, sun, sand and wells. The many hours spent training, fighting, working and surviving in the desert enabled strong bonds to be formed between the men and their horses. They relied on each other in a way that perhaps some people could not understand, but for those who lived, breathed and shared with their equine partners, there was a sense of belonging that enabled them to remain human. Some men were constantly in the saddle. The horses proved that they could move in deep sand, carry 100kg on their backs and go for long periods—many hours and sometimes days—without water. Usually they needed twenty litres a day to keep condition.

The stream of men on horseback moved silently. Guy Powles of the NZ Mounted Rifles captured the atmosphere of the Desert Mounted Column at night when he commented, "Over the swelling sand hills they came, line upon line...no song, no laughter, no talking, not a light to be seen; no sound but the snort of a horse as he blows the dust from his nostrils; or the click of stirrup irons touching as two riders close in together... no other sound is heard unless one be very close, then there is a low swish, swish as the sand spurts out in front of a horse's foot slithering on from step to step."

Among the men there was an unwritten code that 'no sound man would allow himself to be taken prisoner, no wounded man should be left behind to fall into the hands of the enemy.' The men made every effort to get to their wounded mates. The wounded were generally transported by camels using sand carts and sledges, but most preferred to be carried out by mates, or on their own horse. A Desert Mounted Corps Memorial in Canberra reflects this unwritten code, depicting a mounted Australian Light Horseman defending a New Zealander who stands beside his wounded horse.

Camel Corps

The crucial role of the Camel Corps needs to be acknowledged. Not only did they carry essential items but they also carried machine guns. In January 1916 four companies were formed, the 1st and 3rd Australian, 2nd British and 4th Australian/New Zealand. The cameleers of the Australian Camel Corps numbered 2800 men. They went on long patrols in late 1916 alongside the Australian Light Horse in Romani, Magdhaba and Rafa. The camels served as 'the trucks of the desert,' and carried water, food and equipment. Convoys delivered water for men and horses in 'fanatis'—metal containers. Many desert battles were won with the help of camels. They could carry 160kg, go six days without water in the desert and in sand could travel faster than horses. Each camel could carry five days' water supply, rations and camp gear. Their role in evacuating casualties, ferrying patients many miles to the rear, not only the wounded but the sick, was amazing. They were crucial in the Sinai Desert, though their nickname among Australian forces, 'the hooshter* brigade' made light of their worth. The following poem highlights the understating attitude of the Australians:

Our Camel Corps Cobbers

Look at 'em! Cheer at 'em!
Swinging along, Devil-may-cares in a mob,
On ships of the desert all lanky and long
But a dinkum old crew for the "job".

Look at 'em! 'Ark at 'em!
Swinging along,
Their "hooshters" a'skimming the sand; ...[but]
Riding a "hooshter" or riding a horse,
We're one and the same in the line...

In 1917 and '18 the troops advanced through Palestine. The Camel Corps came into its own at Magdhaba in December 1916 and Rafa in 1917. "It will be a long time before eye-witnesses forget that long line of dismounted cameleers that charged towards the Turkish trenches at Rafa, laughing, smoking and jesting," one witness commented.

Top: Wounded or sick Light Horsemen lie in cacolets—camel transports—ready to be taken for treatment.

Above: Sinai January 1918, Australian Camel Corp members in the sands of Rafa.

* The term 'hooshter' came from the cry of 'hooshta!' used to urge the camels forward.

The corps would be disbanded about eighteen months later in June 1918 as the more fertile country in North Palestine was suitable for the faster horses. At that time the cameleers were given horses and became the 14th and 15th Light Horse Regiments. Others went into the 5th Light Horse Brigade.

Desert push

The Light Horse continued the desert push, and their battles along the narrow coastal plain echoed the battles of armies for 2000 years. This was an ancient caravan trail from Palestine to Egypt. It started at the Syrian capital of Damascus, went south to Jerusalem, down to Rafa, through the deserts of North Sinai, all the way to Kantara on the Canal. It followed the ancient wells, so vital to survival in the region.

After a long night march of 80 kilometres, they captured El Arish on the coast on 20 December 1916. El Arish is on the edge of what was the Sinai border with Palestine. The Turkish would go this way along the coast to reach Suez via the wells of Katia and Romani. Chauvel's Anzac Mounted Brigade consisted of the 1st and 3rd Light Horse Brigades, the New Zealand Mounted Rifles, three battalions of the Imperial Camel Brigade and three British infantry battalions.

They moved inland and after another night march of about thirty kilometres on the Plain of Sharon, reached Maghdaba at dawn on 23 December. Here occurred the second major battle—and one of the most successful battles of the war. The troopers fought all day in the scorching sun until sunset. Brigadier Charles Cox, who was leading the attack, had been ordered to retreat as the attack dragged on. He refused. He knew he could win. They fixed bayonets and charged. Trooper Oliver Hogue said, "A small amount dismounted and the cavalry, armed only with rifle and bayonet, charged the open ground and captured the strong fortress." This fortress was protected by six fortified redoubts which surrounded the town. This was an incredible achievement and Royston, hero of Romani, became a legend at Magdhaba also. He organised elements of the 10th regiment in an elaborate bluff which climaxed with his personally leading a charge of the pack leaders and men who were supposed to be holding the led horses. Banjo Paterson

Map showing battle towns of Romani, Maghdaba and Rafa.

Making camp as a dust storm passes over.

A line of dismounted Light Horse troopers advance on Maghdaba, 23 December 1916.

Cartoon drawn on the wall of a building in Maghdaba depicting a Light Horse trooper, a kangaroo and a surrendering enemy soldier.

summed up that Royston was "by instinct a bandit chief and by temperament a hero".

The 2000 entrenched Turks had been in a good position but were surrounded.

The battle of Magdhaba was another success for the Light Horse as casualties were few and they managed to capture 100 guns and take 1200 prisoners. They rode back from Magdhaba to El Arish and arrived at dawn on 24 December after riding close to fifty kilometres in dust storms. In just over twenty-four hours, the Desert Column had ridden eighty kilometres, fought mounted and dismounted, and crushed a strongly fortified enemy.

Australian troopers captured a Turkish flag during the battle of Maghdaba.
(Photo by George Auchterlonie, 8th Light Horse Regiment, 1916)

What the troopers hated most on these long marches were snipers: a lurking terror, an unseen and unheard foe. They fired when the troopers had little cover and often killed their horses. The screams of dying horses sent chills through the men.

Sled stretcher invented by the Australians to transport the wounded.

Conditions for horses in the desert contrasted greatly to those in Europe. The desert offered flies, thirst, fatigue and heat. Europe offered mud, barbed wire, bombardments and bullets— and for little gain, as at that point the war in Europe was at a stalemate. In contrast, the horses in the desert had travelled many kilometres for many victories. At the close of

The horses were watered in portable canvas troughs.

1916, the men who had served at Gallipoli a year earlier would have felt that they had had some revenge on the Turks because they had won several decisive battles. The victories in the Middle East were important and drew relatively few casualties. The Waler horses proved to be the secret weapon in the harsh conditions of the desert campaign. The capacity of these horses to continue working, especially as they often refused food in intense heat, was amazing.

Trooper Ion Idriess wrote in his diary that the constant search for water and wells was fraught with danger as the Turks would often lie in wait ready with machinegun fire. It was often so hot that the men's rifles would burn their skin. At one well the men and horses were so thirsty that "we formed a determined post around that well and I don't think all the Turks out of Hades could have taken water from us".

Aerial bombings were a constant threat and the men took great care to get the wounded out to avoid their becoming prisoners or falling to the Bedouins. To do this, they rigged up the sand cart to take them to safety.

To the British, the Arabs and the Turks, the Australians seemed laid back and uncouth, yet they were fierce when charging, and were helped by their horses adapting well to the dreadful desert conditions. They could "survive on a quart bottle of water per man a day and were well trained and cunning." Their ability to sum up a situation and act was crucial to their survival and their horses were tough.

The Turks called the Australians 'White Ghurkas' because of their deadly skill with the bayonet. The Arabs called them 'Kings of Feathers', while they often referred to themselves 'Billjims,' a colloquial term meaning just ordinary blokes, Bill and Jim.

Another observer said of the Light Horsemen, "They were tired-looking as they moved around with the slouching gait of the Australian country man at home," but when battle was imminent, "it changes into a livesome athletic swing that takes him over the ground much quicker than other troops."[9]

9 Robert Collister Cowley, '7th Australian Light Horse Regiment, 2nd Australian Light Horse Brigade – Beersheba, Es Salt, Damascus', *My Family History*.

7

The Push to Palestine, 1917

'The leading men began standing in their stirrups. The horses started snatching at green grass.'

The huge contingent of Light Horse was reorganised by General Murray into the Desert Column in early 1917, led by Lieutenant General Philip Chetwode. It consisted of the Imperial Mounted Division led by Major-General Henry Hodgson with the 3rd and 4th Australian Light Horse Brigades and the 5th and 6th Yeomanry, and the Anzac Mounted led by Major-General Harry Chauvel with the 1st and 2nd Australian Light Horse Brigades and NZ Mounted Rifles.

BATTLE OF RAFA, 9 January 1917

Two weeks after the success at Magdhaba, on a bitter winter's day—9 January 1917—the 1st and 3rd Light Horse with the NZ Rifles stormed into Rafa, a fortified city close to the border with Palestine. The city was surrounded by a group of Turkish trenches and earth mounds, with open plains leading to it. The strategy was to encircle the city from the open ground, then draw the ring tight. It was 'Galloping Jack' Royston who was instrumental in circling and taking Rafa. The Light Horse and Cameleers moved silently to circle around a sleeping town before first light. They then made galloping dashes followed by the men dismounting and fighting. The excitement for both man and horse to gallop freely across the plain must have been exhilarating. The NZ Mounted Rifles continued the assaults when the other soldiers were preparing to concede. This was a pivotal moment in the attack, and by sunset they had victory. They had encircled 2000 embattled Turks in the third and final battle to complete the recapture of the Sinai Peninsula, before moving on to fight in Palestine.

Lt-Colonel Guy Powles, NZ Rifles, on his trusty horse, Bess, took many photos of the Desert Column's march on Rafa. He wrote, "the leading men began standing in

Picture from album of Lt-Colonel Thomas Joseph Daly

The Australian Light Horse 3rd Brigade marches from El Arish towards Rafa, following the shoreline of the Mediterranean Sea.

The 2nd Light Horse Regiment charges over a ridge in extended order into direct view of enemy redoubts during the Battle of Rafa, 9 January 1917.

their stirrups, waving their hats and pointing ahead...the horses started snatching at green grass...the jaded riders were intoxicated and it was all they could do to keep their mounts going forward with their heads up."

The exhausted troops celebrated with a race meeting in March 1917 dubbed the 'Rafa Races'. Chauvel understood the role of special events such as race meetings in boosting the morale of the battle weary. The program included the 'Anzac Steeplechase', 'the Syrian Derby, the 'Promised Land Stakes,' the 'Border Plate', and the 'Jerusalem Scurry' for mules. General Chauvel wrote to his wife, "We have had a great day today—the Races at Rafa—and I don't know when I have enjoyed a day's racing so much. The course was lovely—beautiful green grass in a large natural amphitheatre—right in the middle of the battlefield of Rafa! The Turks' trenches and rifle-pits need a little dodging when laying out a course, but that was all, and the jumps were sandbag walls with brushwood on top. My own horse, Bally, ran third in the Anzac Steeplechase. I ran him in my groom's name, as I was giving the cup."[10]

This was a unique race meeting as nearly every horse competing had carried its owner in the battle fought where they were now racing.

Sinai

The 2nd Light Horse Brigade stayed in the Sinai policing conquered territory and guarding an advancing railway and water pipe that were under construction through to Rafa. They had cleared the Turkish from Egyptian territory and now the Light Horse marched to Palestine along the desert battle paths that Napoleon, the Crusaders, Ancient Romans and Egyptians had trod before. They were moving across biblical lands to Palestine. Oases stretched along 'the oldest road in the world', and the troopers were awestruck by the sights and sense of history. The Palestine terrain suited the horses better as it was firm ground, similar to outback parts of Australia. "The horses, despite their large loads, were touched with excitement, as they always were marching in large bodies," wrote historian Henry Gullett. It was some relief from the scorching, sinking sands of the Sinai.

The British were surprised by the successes at Magdhaba and Rafa. They now wanted to conquer Palestine. There was a fortified defensive line from Gaza on the coast to Beersheba inland. General Murray was directing the push from afar, back in Cairo. He had enlisted the help of Lieutenant T E Lawrence (Lawrence of Arabia) to encourage the Arabs to revolt and to evict the Turks also.

The push now involved attacking Gaza. One of the oldest cities in the world, Gaza was a powerful fortress in what was Palestine. It is steeped in history, being the setting for the Biblical story of Samson and Delilah. In 332BC, Alexander the Great took the

10 Harry Chauvel, Chauvel War Books (Vol. II), p6

city after a historic siege. Its principal defence feature was a thick maze of tall, prickly cactus hedges all around. This vegetation was hard to ride through and find your targets, and snipers took advantage of this. With 40,000 inhabitants and fortified by Turkish troops, Gaza posed a huge obstacle to the Desert Column with mounted infantry.

Gaza

On 26 March 1917, at 2.30am, amid thick fog, the advance on Gaza commenced. The infantry fought ferociously, supported by artillery attack. The Turkish troops were buried in the redoubts* and they held even after heavy artillery attacks. The Australian Light Horse was sent in. Men went three nights with no sleep and the horses had not been watered; morale was low. Although the Light Horse gained the city, Murray had received reports that Turkish recruitments were on their way so he ordered the men to retreat. There were in fact no Turkish reinforcements, so the Turks were able to regroup and fortify the city. The men could have taken Gaza.

The second attack on Gaza was ordered for 19 April 1917. The order was for a frontal attack. The charge of the Camel Corps on this date against superior numbers will live in history. It was a disaster also, with 6444 British losses and the 10th Light Horse badly afflicted. The artillery attacks and shellings were relentless. "With what extraordinary fortitude our horses stood that infernal racket," wrote Idriess. When horses were hit or blown to bits, their agony penetrated their riders. "Horses scream frightfully when in agony. No matter what hail of death is around a man, he sort of forgets his own peril when an unexplained fear shivers through him when horses scream like that," he said.

After two disastrous attacks on Gaza, many deaths and misinformation from the British leaders, the disheartened soldiers were forced to wait for further orders. Any belief that the war in the desert was not as horrific as the war in the trenches is dispelled by a poem titled *Lucky Tim*, written by 'Trooper Blue Gum' (Oliver Hogue) after the disastrous attacks.

> *At Gaza's heights the Light Horse dashed,*
> *Bold Cameleers charged in vain;*
> *The Welsh were slaughtered, Scots were smashed;*
> *In the Wadi, blood flowed like rain.*
> *Then Tim heard an officer – who at Mons*
> *Had stemmed the Hun's advance –*
> *Exclaim, 'mid the roar of the murdering guns,*
> *'I wish I was back in France.'*

*redoubt: a temporary defensive stronghold.

Shellal mosaic

Above left: The Shellal mosaic in situ, being cleaned and prepared for removal.
Above right: pieces are packed in boxes ready for transportation.

It was during the second attack on Gaza that a group of Australian signalmen, led by Corporal Ernest Lovell-Shore, made a major archaeological discovery at a place called Wadi Guzzi, a few kilometres from Gaza. The floor of a Byzantine church built in 622 AD had become partly exposed by Turkish troops digging a trench. It was a magnificent, colourful Byzantine mosaic depicting tiger, elephant, stag, rabbit, peacocks. It became known as the Shellal Mosaic for the nearby town of Shellal. The precious find was carefully dug up and placed in boxes. Transported to Australia, it is preserved in the Australian War Memorial in Canberra. The War Memorial notes that today, removal of items by personnel serving overseas is not permitted and such an artefact would not now be accepted into its collection, but at the

A detail of the Shellal mosaic stuck onto a wall of the Australian War Memorial in Canberra.

State Library of New South Wales

Hand-coloured photo of the Light Horse halt at Wadi Guzzi, a few kilometres from Gaza.

time, what an amazing find for the soldiers in the middle of a bitter conflict and a reminder about the rich history of the area. Discussions about returning the Shellac Mosaic to the Middle East have been held but the War Memorial has noted any repatriation is politically complex and also risks damaging the mosaic further, as it was glued on to a structural wall in the War Memorial in 1941.

Build-up to Beersheba

For five months there was gridlock for fifty kilometres between Gaza on the coast and Beersheba inland; 20,000 to 25,000 Turks were fully entrenched.

Harry Chauvel was frustrated with having to wait. He wanted to chase and wipe out the enemy, yet his commander, General Murray, seemed reluctant to attack on a grand scale and thereby allowed the Turkish forces to regroup after each battle. The fact that he was not at the battle front and relied on information sent to him may have contributed to this attitude. This all changed when General Allenby ('The Bull') took over from Murray on June 28. Allenby was angry about being taken from the Front. He intended to lead from the desert, not from Cairo. He knew AB Paterson and Harry Chauvel from the Boer War and appointed Chauvel in charge of the massive horse contingent in the desert. He had heard about Bill the Bastard and wanted him for his own mount, but Chauvel told him that Bill was not there. There were heated words and Allenby was heard to say, "...don't go for your Walers much, they're a common, hairy lot compared to the horses the Lancers had in the Boer War." He then said, "this motley lot won't win a war, either!" Paterson had to correct him that they had been a huge factor in defeating the Turks six times in the Sinai already. Allenby refused to concede and commented, "thoroughbreds perform better. Breeding is everything." He had noticed Paterson's own horses and told him that they belonged to the British Army.

Allenby combined all the mounted cavalry, the Desert Column, into a corps in July 1917 and renamed it the Desert Corps. This was to be the largest cavalry ever used in an advance by a British Army. He appointed the Australian General Chauvel in charge of all the mounted units in this Corps—more than 34,000 horsemen. The plan was for the Corps to attack Beersheba, not Gaza. But to achieve success, the strategy was to convince the Turks that Gaza would be attacked, while they would perform a secondary attack on Beersheba. The ruse involved the military head of British Intelligence, Colonel Richard Meinertzhagen, whose plan was to drop a bag containing papers which ordered an attack on Gaza in late November. To convince the Turks of the authenticity of the contents, he included a letter written by his wife saying how much she and their new baby missed him. The British needed the wells in Beersheba to water 60,000 men and tens of thousands of animals—horses, donkeys and camels. Allenby knew they had to break the Turkish hold on Gaza on the coast so they could drive the enemy from Palestine. Taking Beersheba, seventy kilometres south of Gaza, would enable a third and decisive attack on Gaza from the desert.

General Allenby

The push to Palestine 1917

State Library of New South Wales

A long line of troopers snakes back into the distance in this hand-coloured photo of the Light Horse on the march in 1917.

8

Beersheba, 31 October 1917

'The sound of thousands of hoof beats on the desert sand.'
'courage, hunger, thirst, sand, love, trust.'

The troops had been on the march for a few days and arrived at the tiny outpost of Asluj on 30 October. Corporal Harold Gleeson of 12th Light Horse mentions in his diary that they obtained no water there and continued on to Beersheba, marching all night on a wearing and dusty ride.

On 31 October at 5.55am, after a forty-kilometre night ride, the assault on Beersheba from the south-west began and it continued all day. The Australians and New Zealanders had to advance across open ground against two strongly defended hill forts. Mention of heroics of the NZ Mounted Rifles is made by Ion Idriess. "The NZ Mounted Rifles having a hard fight to take the Tel el Saba redoubts on a high hill," he wrote. It was the original site of the ancient city and was still in Turkish hands even after bombardments. "Snipers rained down bullets from above. Capturing it was vital. "The machine-gun fire just roared from down there, our artillery all along the line were thundering at the German machine-gun nests," Idriess said.

Fighting lasted into the late afternoon and about 2 or 3pm the two forts fell, thanks in part to the heroic actions of Staff Sergeant Jack Cox, from Bendigo, Victoria. His 4th Light Horse had nearly surrounded the line of machine gunners when Cox saw Turks assembling a machine gun, setting it up to fire at close range from the side of the advancing horsemen. He knew what carnage it could do so he turned his galloping horse at right angles and charged towards them, waving his revolver and screaming. His charge worked. The forty machine gunners surrendered and many lives were saved. He was later recommended for a VC but was given a distinguished conduct medal instead.

His effort epitomised the Australian sense of doing what was needed even if it meant danger to themselves.

While this was a great result, the trenches protecting the town were still heavily defended. Despite artillery and air support neither the infantry attacks from the south or the Anzac Mounted Division from the east succeeded.

There was about an hour of daylight left. The riders knew that there was no water available until Beersheba fell into their hands. The 4th Light Horse Brigade was ordered to take the town. Time was running out and Lieutenant General Harry Chauvel had been ordered by Allenby to charge close to the trenches, dismount and make their attack on foot. Chauvel waited until he felt the time was right and instead of ordering the charge as per Allenby's orders, he ordered a charge without stopping. Chauvel had great confidence in his leader of the 4th Brigade, Brigadier Grant.

About 4.30pm, by which time the horses had been without water for 48 hours, he said, "Put Grant straight at them." The order "Mount up," was given to Grant and his 4th Light Horse Brigade. The Victorian 4th Regiment, led by William Bourchier, and the NSW 12th Regiment, led by Cameron—together 800 men and horses—were to charge at dusk, within about 15 minutes. Grant was fully aware of the immense

MOVING TOWARDS BEERSHEBA

4th Light Horse on the way to take part in the attack on Beersheba.

Advancing towards Beersheba prior to the final charge; the hateful dust clearly visible.

responsibility he had and addressed the men. "You're fighting for water. There's no water between this side of Beersheba and Esani. Use your bayonets as swords. I wish you the best of luck."

As Gullet wote, "surprise and speed were their one chance".

And so the 4th and the 12th, with the 11th in reserve, came over the ridge from the north and north-east, set for the charge. The men were excited, but afraid, and their horses were on edge also. The Germans in charge of Beersheba's defence were convinced that it was a demonstration and believed that the Australians would dismount.

The horses formed three lines up to half a kilometre apart and each over a kilometre long. The troopers' bayonets were in their hands, like swords. The 4th regiment was on the right and the 12th was on the left. Ahead of them was a three-kilometre mounted charge over open ground against trenches, artillery and machine guns. Turkish field commanders would later report that they thought it was a joke, crazed horsemen charging into the barrels of trenched machine guns, backed by the world's largest guns. The Light Horse began at a walk then walk-march, then trot, then canter. About two kilometres from the trenches, Brigadier Grant flexed his arm and extended it towards Beersheba, and bellowed, "Forward!" The men galloped towards the trenches in the dying sunlight. The Turkish machine guns opened fire and German planes dropped bombs. The Turks expected the Light Horse to stop, dismount and charge on foot and so did not lower their gun sights. The Turkish-German forces numbered 4400 and the odds were against the Light Horse.

They were galloping, "the boys were wild-eyed and yelling their heads off," trooper Martin Balsarini later described; "they went in like the hounds of Hell."

They were probably frightened, but as Ion Idriess wrote, "I think all men get scared at times like these but there comes a sort of laughing courage from deep within the heart of each, or some source he never knew existed; and when he feels like that he will gallop into the most blinding death with an unexplainable, don't care, shrieking laugh upon his lips."

One mile ahead, a British trooper, Eric Elliot, was hidden on a small rise, looking through binoculars and trying to spot enemy positions for Allied artillery. He heard the thunder of galloping horses, turned, and was so shocked he dropped his binoculars. He had just enough time to get on his horse and get out of the way. Elliot would later recall "It was the bravest, most awe-inspiring sight I ever witnessed, and there they were... yelling, swearing and shouting. There were more than 500 Aussie horsemen .... As they thundered past my hair stood on end."

The men lay flat along the horses' necks, the horses at full gallop. One trooper wrote of "...the sound of thousands of hoof beats on the desert sand, the sweat, the leather, men and animals being hit and then into the trench line. Close up, hand to hand stuff."

Idriess in *The Desert Column* commented, "the berserk gallop of the Light Horse and their mad shouts as they feveriously attacked the Turkish trenches that day echoed through the hills. They were an awe-inspiring sight, galloping through the red haze—knee to knee and horse to horse—the dying sun glinting on bayonet points."

Hand-to-hand fighting erupted after riders gained the trenches. Horses were bayoneted from below as they leapt over the trenches. The sounds of thundering hooves, screaming horses and dying men filled the air. Brigadier Murray Bourchier of the 4th Light Horse led his squadron on the left and was later commended for "... his skilful handling of his Regiment and by his magnificent example of courage and determination, was very largely instrumental in the success of the attack and capture of the town." He shot six Turks when he reached the trenches, and dismounted for hand-to-hand fighting.

Trooper Edward Dengate of the 4th later commented, "we spurred our horses...the bullets got thicker...three or four horses came down, others with no riders kept on going, their saddles splashed with blood."

The field ambulances came after to find fallen troopers. Bill the Bastard was used to carry one young trooper, Towers, to safety. As Towers lay dying in agony he asked after his Waler and Bill the Bastard. He then told other troopers that his name was really Ben Burke, and he was only seventeen. He had been fourteen when he joined up in 1914.*

*The real story of Trooper Towers

It turned out that the young trooper Towers had met Bill the Bastard before.

According to Roland Perry's book *Bill the Bastard*, when Towers volunteered at Liverpool Army Camp horse yards to serve in the Australian Light Horse, he stated his age as 17, but the recruiting officer was sceptical.

"Break out Bill for Mr Towers," was the direction. Everyone around the yards knew that Bill was used as a test of the horsemanship skills of underage recruits. Anyone who could stay on Bill for any length of time was considered a good rider and recruiting staff often turned a blind eye to their age.

Towers was the first rider ever to stay on Bill for over two minutes. The recruiting officer advised Towers to go for a walk around the block and come back a year older.

The Light Horse gallops across the plain near Beersheba. Debate has surrounded this photograph since soon after the war ended. Some investigators believe it is the actual charge of 31 October 1917, photographed by Trooper Eric Elliot who described

Beersheba, 31 October 1917

taking such a photo, others that it is a re-enactment staged in February 1918 by photographer Frank Hurley. With no defiitive proof either way, the official standpoint of the Australian War Memorial is that the photo depicts the reenactment.

Thirty-one from the Light Horse were killed and 36 wounded. Seventry horses were killed and over 60 wounded.

The charge at Beersheba was considered the most successful large-scale charge in the previous 200 years. The Ottoman lines had held all day and it was only the late, desperate charge that finally shattered their lines.

The wells in Beersheba had been mined to prevent the British from accessing the water. German officers were in the process of blowing them up when the Australians charged. Trooper Sloan 'Scotty' Bolton followed some wires and stopped the German officer at the switchboard and saved the wells, bar two or three that had been blown up. By 7pm, 60,000 men and 100,000 animals descended on Beersheba.

The prime concern after this success was watering the thousands of horses. Many had already gone 48 hours without water and had performed while suffering severely from thirst. "It was worth a month's pay to see old Charley stick his head down, and drink, and drink, and drink," wrote one soldier. Controlling the horses was difficult. "When they saw the water, they threw themselves on their knees and upset as much as they drank," one trooper commented. Another: "some horses rushed forward uncontrollably when they smelt the water, unsettling the troughs."

Water was crucial to success and it was distressing to see horses collapse from the lack of water. "One animal lay down and seemed close to death, until someone gave him a drink of water," a trooper later wrote. "He struggled to his feet and drank it out of a dixie lid*."

Over the next two days they had to carry out small attacks to the north and east of Beersheba to secure further sources of water.

The concern for their horses is paramount to understanding the feats of the Australian riders.

Guy Haydon on Midnight

*Dixie – trench slang for tin pot used for cooking

This story is told of Lieutenant Guy Haydon of the 12th Light Horse: Haydon was a gun polo player and he had ridden his black mare, Midnight, since he was a boy. Midnight came over with him when he joined up. Haydon was separated from Midnight when he was sent to Gallipoli. When he returned to Egypt, he found she had been given to another trooper. He searched high and low until he found her. A fellow trooper had recognised the Haydon brand on her near shoulder and he arranged a swap so he could have her back. Haydon was part of the desert assault and was at the failed second battle for Gaza. At that stage he had ridden Midnight for seven days continuously. He was involved in the charge at Beersheba. As he led his men, riding Midnight, over a trench, a Turkish bullet went through her body and into Haydon. Midnight was mortally wounded. The Lieutenant had a bullet lodged in his back. He lay there wounded and completely devastated next to the body of his beloved Midnight. He survived this battle but the injury led to his return to

Depiction of the scene at Beersheba in which Midnight ridden by Tpr Guy Haydon was killed, by Jennifer Marshall.

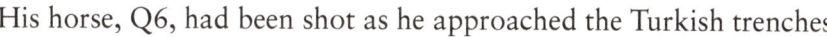

Trooper Len Hall

Australia. He had been with his horse as a constant companion for three years during the desert assault and they had been together for a total of twelve years. Haydon's love for his horse was part of his existence.

The last surviving rider from the Beersheba charge, machine gunner Len Hall, said of the charge, "that was what we had been trained for. I felt quite naked without my horse, which I had got from the cattle baron Sid Kidman. And although we fought well at Gallipoli and survived that bloody massacre at the Nek, we could not wait to show what we could do once we were reunited with our horses."

His horse, Q6, had been shot as he approached the Turkish trenches.

"When he fell under me, I jumped clear quick smart to see if I could save him but he was a goner, so I had to shoot him through the head," said Hall. "Even in the middle of the battle with blokes dying all around me, I broke down and wept for Q6 as I'd lost the best friend I ever had."

Hall, a horse driver from Nungarin in WA, had nudged his age up a bit to be able to enlist in 1914; he was actually 17 at the time.

When Allenby met Chauvel after hearing of the success at Beersheba he asked how the troopers had got across the enemy trenches. Chauvel replied, "we just jumped the bastards". Many horses received terrible injuries when the Turks lifted their bayonets to the horses' bellies as they jumped over them. The horses were also hit by bullets. One Light Horseman recounted that, "there was nothing more sickening than the sound of bullets thudding into the belly of your horse." About 70 horses were killed and more were wounded or became sick afterwards, having been in a bad state after their long ride and with little or no water for close to two days.

One hero of Beersheba was Major Cuthbert Fetherstonhaugh, a grazier from NSW. He epitomised the troopers' dedication to each other and their horses. He was with his squadron when he came to the enemy trenches under heavy rifle and machinegun fire. He charged full at the trenches, joining the leading squadron. His horse was shot from under him thirty-odd metres from the trench but he still led his men forward on foot and using his revolver, and they overcame the enemy troops.

Major Cuthbert Fethersonhaugh by George Lambert, 1918.

Charles Bean wrote, "A South African veteran and fine soldier, his first thought was for his wounded horse and he quickly put it out of pain with one shot from his revolver before rushing to the trench, shot a Turk before falling, shot through both legs."

"In the long months of desert fighting and this fighting in Palestine, there had come into being an interdependence of horse and rider quite beyond what Lord Methuen meant in the Royal Commission on the War in South Africa, when he said—as regards the Colonial Corps—the rider and his horse were one."

The capture of Beersheba turned the tide for the allied forces in Palestine.

9

The push north
November 1917- January 1918

Winter.
"I shall never forget the horror of that ride—slipping, sliding, crawling from ledge to ledge."

With the fall of Gaza on 7 November 1917, the Turkish position in south Palestine collapsed. By November-December, the Turkish forces were pushed back. There were many bitter fights and one New Zealand soldier from the Anzac Division recalled his horse Flame's loyalty: "We couldn't have won this war without the horses. Flame saved my life more than once," he later said. This great partnership between man and horse continued as the great mounted army moved northwards towards Jerusalem. All eyes were now on Jerusalem.

Jerusalem sat high up in the Judean Hills. As the bitter winter set in, the Desert Mounted Corps found the going tough. They endured long treks over the stony hills. The tracks were narrow. Through these rugged mountains the men even climbed on hands and knees over wet, slippery rocks, any soil moving away in the torrents of rain. Lt-Colonel Arthur Olden, WA 10th Regiment, commented, "the plucky horses would follow them like well-trained dogs".

From November 19 to 21 it rained in torrents. It was bitterly cold and men and horses suffered. There was no firewood, only mud and slush. The troopers camped in caves and rock shelters. They huddled for warmth and protection with their horses,

The rocky, difficult terrain of the Judean Hills.

sharing the freezing conditions in the bleak hills with their 'mates'. There were bare ridges and no escape from the biting winds, rain and sometimes frostbite.

Jerusalem, the Holy City, has been claimed by three major religions: Judaism, Islam and Christianity. The Crusades saw bitter conflict between Christians and Muslims, and finally the Ottoman Empire had held control for the past 600 years when World War One broke out. The significance of this history was uppermost in Christians' minds and the Australian Light Horse were about to lead the march to win back the city and free it from Turkish rule.

On the night of 7 December, a huge storm broke. Torrential rain fell from 7 to 9 December so conditions were treacherous. The plain became a bog: the horses sank to their bellies, and in the lines they stood hock deep in mud, and miserable.

Brigadier General Charles Cox leads a regiment of the Australian Light Horse near Jerusalem, February 1918. Picture Frank Hurley collection

The 10th Light Horse from WA led by Olden was given the honour of entering Jerusalem and liberating it from Turkish rule. Chauvel had selected the 10th as he saw they needed healing after the disastrous attack at the Nek at Gallipoli. They had also suffered losses at Hill 60 on the Western Front in August 1915. Lt. Hugo Throssell won a Victoria Cross at this battle. He was the only Australian Light Horseman to do so. The 10th also fought at Romani and Magdhaba and on the Beersheba-Gaza lines.

On 8 December they attacked and by 9 December they had conquered and then left Jerusalem. What an awe-inspiring sight it must have been watching the Light Horse columns winding their way from the city.

Trooper Bill Griffiths spent Christmas in the Judean Hills and it rained for days. "Everyone was soaked to the skin because a woollen blanket and greatcoat were of little protection," he later commented. "Judea was a desolation of rocks and bare stone hills," he wrote. "A carcass of a land." Horses needed to be clipped so they would dry off more quickly and not get chills, and many were in poor condition, needing shoes, and many also suffered from strangles. The narrow steep tracks over the hills could only be traversed single file and dismounted. The high cliffs and zig-zag track led down to the flat Jordan Valley where the Jordan River flowed.

Jordan 1918

Colonel Olden, in his book *They Rode Into History*, paid tribute to the horses.

"One can only marvel at the extraordinary adaptability and courage of the Australian horses," he wrote. "They climbed and descended impossible looking hills and ravines with the agility of mountain goats. By no means starved, they had many times been short of food; they were leg-weary and shin sore, carried heavy loads through blinding red dust of Beersheba, then over rubble and rocks of Judean Hills, and finally through torrential winter rain-storms and bogs, mud and slush. They had not decently rested themselves for weeks, and—what is much to a horse—they had not had a decent roll. Now, they rolled and rolled, and kept on rolling…"

The troops had some relief from the narrow, rocky tracks of the hills when they were able to camp in the Jordan Valley for a couple of months during February and March. However it was freezing cold and they encountered many problems with the horses; many were now unfit and the regiment needed replacements.

To ward off the cold and boredom, the troopers held camp competitions featuring horse racing and show jumping. One huge event, the 'Australian Mounted Division Horse Show and Sports' was held on 9 March 1918 in Palestine. Again, this event was crucial to morale and could showcase strength and skill. It was comprised of the mounted tug of war, wrestling on horseback, jumping events, field ambulance competitions, swordsmanship with a bayonet on horseback, races including the 'Palestine Grand National'—in which Chauvel's horse, Bally, came third—and the last event was the officers' three-furlong flutter. There are many funny stories associated with events held on this day. [nb pic of printed program available]

There was even a football game on the Sunday afternoon following the sports weekend.

The push north: November 1917 - January 1918

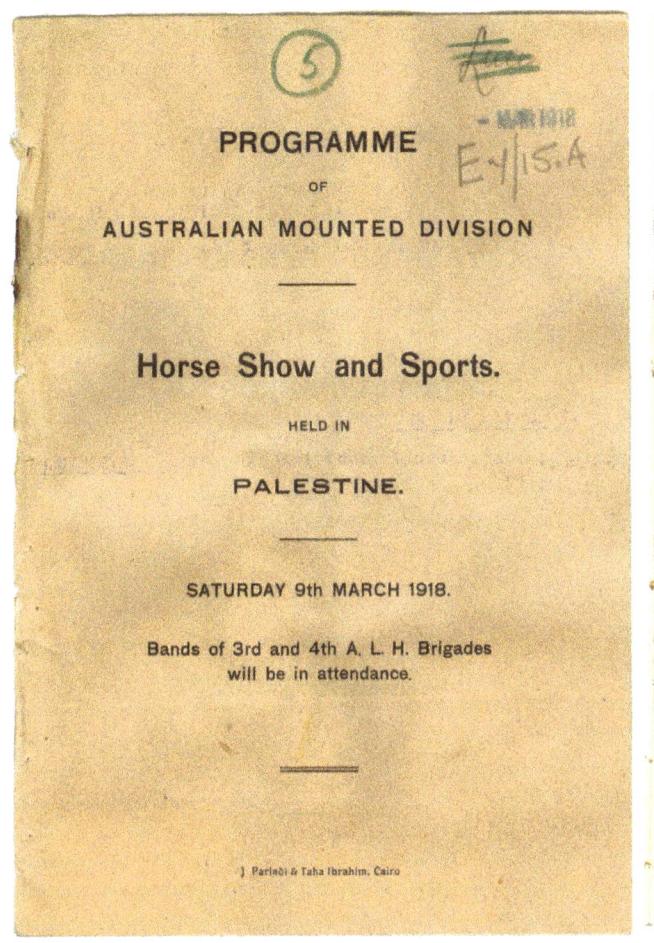

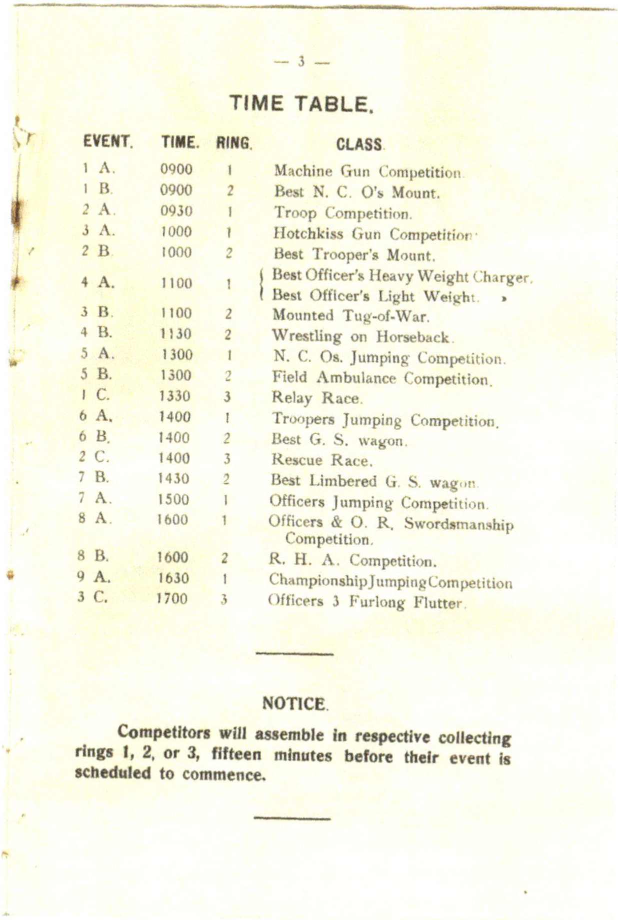

First two pages of the program for morale-boosting sports day held on 9 March 1918.

Horseback wrestling in progress.

Es Salt and Amman
Two fortress towns just north of the Dead Sea
22 March – 4 May 1918

In March 1918 the Anzac Division was ordered to raid Amman, the Jordanian capital, and cut off the Hedjaz railway which was supplying the Turkish army with provisions and guns. Turkish forces fired from a hill that dominated the town. The Anzacs were pushed back. While making their way back through a village, the troopers were fired on by a sniper which caused havoc and many men were wounded. The wounded men were carried on their horses, face down with their heads to the horses' tails. Their hands were tied under the flanks to keep them on the horses. There were 90 to 100 casualties in the 6th Regiment.

> **Amman raid, March 1918**
> A story is told that during the raid on Amman, a young New Zealand trooper's horse, Flame, was shot and the trooper dismounted. "He was told to get out of there, but, 'She needs me—she's hurt,' the trooper said.
>
> "He sat down and cradled Flame's golden head in his lap. Her eyes were wide and frightened, but as he gently stroked her trembling muzzle, they closed."

The Australians were to remain in the Jordan Valley for several months. During this time, they raided Es Salt (30 April to 4 May). Following the Beersheba strategy, they went at full gallop to storm the town. Their actions gained enemy admiration. A German was said to have later commented, "they galloped horses where no-one else would have ridden at all," and a Turkish observer said, "Es Salt has been captured by the reckless and dashing gallantry of the Australian cavalry."

However, conditions were difficult and later the Turks regained control. Brigadier Grant with his 4th and 12th Regiments had to retreat, single file, along the ridges and gorges while the Turks marched on the level plain below. Trooper Alfred Hird from Koondrook in Victoria complained, "I shall never forget the horror of that ride, slipping, sliding, crawling from ledge to ledge."

The 11th Regiment had to fire, gallop to a new position, stop and fire again. At the foothills of Red Hill, they joined the 4th Regiment and held the enemy back. While the raid was a tactical failure, it helped convince the Turks that the next offensive would be launched across the Jordan.

The Anzac Mounted Division remained in the Jordan Valley for the summer months of June, July and August to hold it against the Turks. The Jordan Valley is the lowest place on earth, 400 metres below sea level, and it was hot. The locals call it "the Valley of Death". The men endured extremely tough conditions. "For every gallon of water, you had to drink at Romani, you needed two in the Jordan Valley," said one. The heat did not get below 38 degrees Celsius, and 52 degrees was recorded on several days. Men and horses had to contend with the heat, flies, scorpions up to twelve centimetres long, huge spiders, and snakes. For entertainment, some troopers staged fights between scorpions and tarantulas and the men bet heavily on them.

Bread was dry and hard and the bully beef soft and mushy. The horses' metal shoes heated and scorched their hooves and had to be removed. After three weeks in the valley, the horses could scarcely drag

A section of the 4th Light Horse Brigade stirs up the relentless dust on a patrol in the Jordan Valley.

Dust storm in camp.

themselves the couple of kilometres to water and back. The only relief was to swim in the water when they got there. 'Willy willies' would sweep through the camps and a grey-white dust got into everything. "Sometimes you would sleep all night in a cloud of dust," one man wrote. The troopers hung out with their four-legged friends, grooming and caring for them.

George Auchterlonie, 8th Light Horse, noticed that they were "losing a lot of men with malaria and sand fly fever."* Watching the men suffer with malaria was heartbreaking, he wrote. "It was a tragic sight to see men who had endured so much suddenly stricken, swaying in the saddles and pitching headlong, or lying down for a rest and being unable to rise again."

Enemy planes bombed the camps. There were heavy losses among the horses. This, combined with the physical conditions, sapped the troopers' energy. At one stage, Allenby, insistent that proper dress be maintained, was furious to see the Light Horse riding in shorts in the extreme heat. He ordered full heavy riding kit should be worn at all times or serious consequences would be enforced.

The 4th Light Horse remained behind to protect the pass while the 3rd safely crossed and, dismounted and in single file, climb the other side of the valley.

Australian War Memorial

The Big Push, to culminate in an attack on 19 September along the Plain of Sharon on the Mediterranean coast, was in the planning. It was imperative that the Turks believed the attack would come from the Jordan Valley. As planning continued, news trickled in about progress on the Western Front. On 8-9 August the Battle of Amiens had been masterminded by Colonel John Monash, the brilliant Australian strategist, who used tanks in the offensive. The Germans lost two armies in 48 hours. In effect, this ended the war in Europe.

---

*Sandfly bites caused short-term influenza-like symptoms

GROOMING

Keeping horses well-groomed, even in the dirty conditions of the battlefield, served several purposes. Good grooming standards meant the horses were always prepared for battle at a moment's notice. Grooming also helped to prevent chafing from harnesses and saddles, keeping horses in better condition for longer. At the same time, it gave the carers the opportunity to inspect their horses for pain, wounds or sickness on a daily basis.

Troopers were told to clip their horses to help control skin infections, particularly on the Western Front, and to help them dry off more quickly so they would not get chills. Unfortunately, this led to an increase in the number of animals dying from exposure to in winter months, so the order was relaxed so that only the legs and stomachs were clipped.

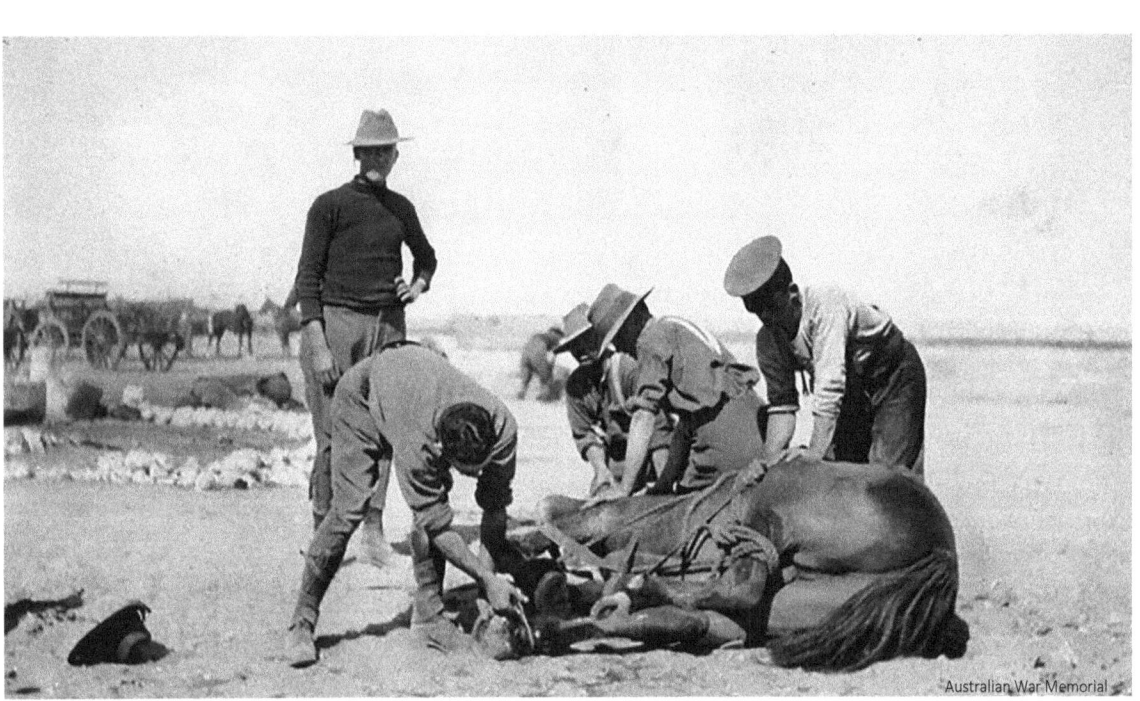

A group of Light Horsemen clip a troublesome horse in Maadi, Egypt, 1915.

Australian War Memorial

Horse clippers came in handy. Three members of the 9th Australian Light Horse pictured in Sinai on 17 August 1917. The soldier on the left is having his hair cut with horse clippers which are being run by a manual air compressor, of which the handle is being rapidly turned by the soldier on the right. The latter has the reins of the horse behind him and an unseen one to the right wrapped around his left wrist.

10
The Great Ruse
September 1918, Syria

"They made 15,000 of these (dummy) horses out of wooden frames, stakes and sticks..."

The Big Push was another major offensive to drive the Turks out of Palestine, Syria and Arabia. It involved Jaffa, a port town by the sea. There were picturesque villages dotted around here with lush orange, apple and almond groves. The area is steeped in history. Crusaders once tied their ships up there and Richard the Lionheart fought Saladin and

Men of the 15 Light Horse regiment, revelling in the freedom of nakedness, swim their horses at Jaffa, Palestine.

Picture: Australian War Memorial

The Great Ruse: September 1918, Syria

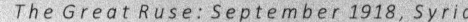

Australian War Memorial

A row of dummy horses at a camp in the Jordan Valley.

the Muslims in the late twelfth century during the Third Crusade. According to legend, Jonah set sail from Jaffa before being swallowed by the whale, and Greek legend tells of Princess Andromeda who was chained to a rock here as a sacrifice to a sea monster.

After the difficult conditions of the Jordan Valley, the proximity of Jaffa to the ocean offered the prospect of some relief for the Australians. On one occasion when near the sea, the troops were crawling with body lice. Their clothes were taken to be treated and they rode bare-back and naked into the sea. What a relief for man and horse, and a rare luxury.

Harry Chauvel secretly planned to move his Australian Mounted Light Horse from the Jordan Valley under cover of darkness and advance around 80 kilometres in the first day and night to the plains near the coast at Jaffa. They would hide in the orange groves while the British Infantry attacked from the east. For this plan to work, it was crucial that the Turks believed the real threat came from the Jordan Valley where the Anzac Mounted Corps was stationed.

To confuse enemy airmen, the troopers set up dummy camps

with empty tents and laid out lines of dummy horses. They made 15,000 of these horses out of wooden frames, stakes and sticks and put real rugs on their backs. Huge piles of horse fodder were dumped near the fake horse lines to maintain the deception. Men rode up and down constantly to create dust and the impression of activity.

To ensure that the Turks believed they were staying in the Jordan Valley and no suspicion was aroused that Jaffa would be attacked, Chauvel organised a five-event race meeting on the outskirts of Jericho on 18 September. The main race was a three-mile (5km) race dubbed the Jericho Cup. Printed programs were distributed in the major towns for 'The Great Horse Show.' Hundreds of horses were entered and the big Australian Walers, including Bill the Bastard, were instant drawcards. Banjo Paterson's own non-Waler Arabian thoroughbreds Khartoum, a big black stallion, Tut 1, a gelding, Tut 2, a stallion and Blackham, a white mare, raced. Khartoum was the out and out favourite and betting was rife on the Jericho Cup—with some good-natured side-betting on how far Bill's rider would get before the big Waler bucked him off.

The first races were all between 1000 and 1700 metres long. Many horses struggled and tragically, in one race, a mare collapsed and died after being bitten by an asp. Another was taken out for treatment after a scorpion bite. The temperature during the day was in the low 30s^c but by 6pm when the Jericho Cup was run it was cooler. Jackie Mullagh, a First Nations horse handler-come-jockey who had been assigned Bill the Bastard after General Shanahan was injured, rode bareback. Many believed he would be quickly bucked off. Mullagh recalled Shanahan's advice on handling the horse given during a long period when Mullagh was slowly getting Bill used to him: "Never dig a stirrup into him. Use a gentle heel. Heel and hands, that's what he responds to. Sweet words of praise in his ear never hurt. He knows your voice. Stroke his mane. You must have an inner rapport with Bill…He has to believe in you…respect his intelligence."

They won the race and it was when they were at the trough to get a drink that Bill bucked Mullagh off. That horse had a mind of its own.

There were more than 10,000 spectators at

Plain of Sharon, today in Israeli coastal plain region.

the race day and it certainly convinced the Turks. Full credit to Harry Chauvel, who was a level-headed leader and well respected. "Chauvel's courage and calmness were matched by his humanity… in the field he lived simply, sleeping in his greatcoat on the sand when his force was on the move," wrote biographer A.J. Hill. Chauvel's plan to fool the Turks was smart and implemented with precision. Attention to detail ensured its success.

The Australian Light Horse was ready by sunset on September 19 to attack Jaffa from the Plain of Sharon. This plains area is steeped in history; it was the scene of battles for centuries, it is mentioned in the Bible, and archaeological evidence has been found of settlements dating back at least 7000 years. In 1918, it was the scene of battle once again.

General Allenby ordered an artillery bombardment and the infantry broke enemy lines. The Light Horse then charged over the plain. The horses knew they were going somewhere fast; rider to horse, horse to horse, they all shared their exuberance, a bond. A trooper later said "A huge body of horsemen spilled over the Plain of Sharon like the flood of a bursting dam." As with the charge at Beersheba, the understanding between horses and their riders was evident when they were to do something dangerous. Banjo Paterson captures this in his poem *Do They Know?* Although the poem is referring to racehorses, it captures the nature of all horses. They know what is happening; the excitement, going fast, being all together: "they snatched at their bits and tossed their heads." They rode through the gap after the retreating Turks.

Meanwhile, the rest of the Anzac Division attacked Amman again and finally captured the town on 25 September. With the Turkish army crushed in this area, the rest of the Desert Corps could concentrate on heading for Damascus in Syria to defeat the remainder of the Turkish forces.

There was sometimes time for fun. Two members of South Australia's 9th Light Horse having smoko with a mate, 1918.

'Not without the horses...'
Above: Troopers stand in reflection at the burial of Sgt Louis Brook and Trooper Clarence Radburn, their saddled horses standing behind the graves, an essential part of the service. Palestine, September 1918.

Three men and a horse, c1916.

Written on the back of this image of unidentified troopers is the proud note, "Three of our best horses." Dated 1917.

Time for smiles: A cheery snap to send back home.

11

The Great Ride
19 September – 1 October 1918

800 kilometres in 12 days

"Such an incredible feat could not have been achieved without the endurance and strength of the Waler."

'The Great Ride' occurred 10 and a half months after the breach of the Gaza-Beersheba line in October 1917. The Desert Corps made up the biggest column of mounted men since Alexander the Great crossed the same deserts. They marched from the Palestine coast, across the Plains of Armageddon into Syria to claim Damascus.

Between 19 and 21 September 1918, 12,000 horses were ridden 90 kilometres in 22 hours—with no sleep for two days and nights—from Jaffa, north up the coast of Palestine, chasing the Turks. The 10th Light Horse led the chase. In these three days, 15,000 prisoners were taken.

During this great ride, one of the last acts of the Light Horse was a battle at Tzemach, near the Sea of Galilee, at a fortified railway complex. On the afternoon of September 24, Brigadier William Grant (4th Light Horse) was given orders by Chauvel to attack Tzemach railway complex at dawn. This complex was very important for communications and as a strategic position. Grant was told there were "a few hundred men with some machine guns"; in fact it had thirteen machine guns set up around its perimeter and the station was heavily fortified with many more than 'a few hundred men'.

What began as a ride in the dark with moonlight as the only illumination, culminated in a dawn attack, 25 September 1918. Two Australian squadrons from the

11th Queensland regiment were involved in this action. This would turn out to be the last cavalry-style charge and the only one during which the Light Horse used drawn swords. Swords were only issued after Beersheba.

When they were two kilometres from the station, they were ordered to form a line and charge. What a shock awaited them when machine guns began firing from concealed bunkers and half the men had their horses shot out from under them during the initial charge. The sound of dying men and horses must have been harrowing. The troopers had to dismount and engage in hand-to-hand combat with swords and bayonets in a short but bitter battle, and acts of bravery undoubtedly contributed to the Australians' success.

Henry Gullet wrote, "...the garrison, outnumbering the Australians by 2 to 1 and made up largely of Germans, had, in addition to their extraordinary position and their machine guns, an ample store of hand grenades."

It was a small but bloody battle, with many Germans killed or wounded and the rest taken prisoner. The Australians suffered deaths, many injuries and the loss of many horses, which caused great anxiety. The Australian machine gunners whose horses hauled the weapons came up after the initial charge and helped rescue the squadrons.

It needs to be noted that there were 30 First Nations troopers in the 11th Regiment, the largest number serving in one unit. Over 1000 First Nations men were granted the right to serve in the army late in the war.

In 2019, a statue titled The Aborigine and His Horse was dedicated in Tzemach—101 years after the fateful battle—in honour of the First Nations soldiers who fought and fell in WWI. The statue is pictured here before it was transported to Tzemach.

Only four days after the amazing feat at Tzemach, an unusual event occurred. On September 29, two squadrons from the 5th Light Horse Regiment surrounded the town of Ziza. There were 4500 Turkish troops there. The Turks agreed to surrender the next day because they were concerned that Arab guerillas in the distance would take the town and slaughter everyone that night, and the 5th Light Horse agreed to protect the Turkish garrison. That night the Turks and the Australians united against the Arabs. In the morning the Turkish force surrendered, as promised.

The Australians respected the Turks somewhat because they were determined and fierce foes. Ion Idriess wrote, "every man in his own fashion—by praise or jest or grim curse—expressed admiration for the willingness, the determination and bitter stubbornness of the Turk."

Within a fortnight, three complete enemy armies were destroyed and 75,000 prisoners were taken. Such an amazing feat could not have been achieved without the incredible endurance and strength of the Walers and the bond between horse and rider: 'one is no good without the other.' Trust and loyalty kept them going. The Desert Mounted Corps undertook a tortuous journey with 12,000 horses, 57,000 troops, and camels, mules and donkeys, across treacherous mountain and desert terrain. They covered 700 kilometres in thirteen days in their push to take Damascus, the last bastion of Turkish defences.

The British officer T.E. Lawrence (Lawrence of Arabia) was leading Arab forces from Aquba in the north. Their purpose was to push the Turkish forces back over the border into Turkey. There were 20,000 Turks in Damascus and its outskirts. General Chauvel's orders were to surround Damascus but not enter unless necessary.

12

Damascus and the end of the war

'It was the horse that did it; those marvellous bloody horses.'

On 1 October 1918, at 5am, the Western Australian 10th Light Horse—800 men—led by Colonel Olden and the 9th Regiment, set out from Barada Gorge thirty kilometres west of Damascus. They stopped a train going through the Gorge and captured 800 Turkish soldiers. They then approached the fort at full gallop. The famed war horse Bill the Bastard was moved to the head of the column and as he galloped at the front he was a fearful sight, seventeen hands of chestnut terror. The 12,000 leaderless Turks did not challenge. The Light Horse thundered into Damascus as conquering heroes.

Outside, the waiting troops were surrounded by a cheering throng. Their horses, used to anything, were reportedly happily accepting grapes and peaches and sweet cakes, "even having flowers fastened in their bridles."[11] Olden put someone in charge and then pursued the Turkish troops who had abandoned the fort. He did not want them to regroup.

Anzac troops had orders not to enter the city unless absolutely forced to do so. But the troops also had orders to isolate the city, and the best way to do it was to march directly through it to block the enemy's escape route, and also to keep order.

On October 1 the Australian troops entered Damascus.

Lawrence of Arabia arrived two hours later and was unhappy that the Australians had got there first; he was concerned that Arabs should get credit for being first into Damascus, since they had been promised they could keep territory they had captured. Lawrence told Chauvel he was concerned the Anzac march through Damascus might

11 *First to Damascus*, 2002, Duchess of Hamilton, p130-31

affect the political future of the city and its role in Arab self-determination.

Wary of the politics, Lawrence would later publish a report that Arab fighters had beaten the Anzacs. The official history was censored by the British. Instead of the news 'Australians first to Damascus' it became 'Entry into Damascus.' Instead of '...the first troops were Australian,' it became 'First British Troops'. The British High Command had ordered this.

Lawrence did not ever meet Chauvel again, but the Australian commander always pointed out who reached Damascus first.

The final stages of the Palestine Campaign 1917-18 were relentless charges at Turkish lines by the Light Horse. War was won in the Middle East theatre and achieved the surrender of Constantinople. The Turkish forces had superior weapons and outnumbered the allied forces, yet could not handle the lightning charges by the mounted horsemen which overran frontline positions in minutes. Lt-General Chauvel and his Light Horse had ridden for three years from Cairo, defeating two Turkish armies in Egypt, Palestine, Lebanon, Syria

General Chauvel leads troops through Damascus, 1 October 1918.

Australian War Memorial

The Australian Light Horse squadrons entering the square in Damascus, 1 October 1918.

and Jordan. There had been 26 major cavalry battles. In particular, between 19 September and 31 October—42 days—80,000 prisoners hd been taken over 800 kilometres with 649 casualties, under torrid conditions: this is certainly something that stays in one's mind.

This extraordinary story of man and his horse is one that should be remembered and due credit and compassion given to the horses. As one Light Horseman would later say, "It was the horses that did it; those marvellous bloody horses. Where would we have been but for them?"

The war in the desert had ended on 31 October 1918. Harry Chauvel's Desert Mounted Column had liberated the Middle East for the first time in 400 years. The war in Europe ended soon after, on 11 November.

While the Light Horse was successful in the Desert Campaign, we should remember the 4th and 13th Light Horse Brigades who remained to serve in Europe, where trench warfare took its toll. They are often forgotten because they rarely fought as complete units, rather supporting British, Canadian and French troops. In 1916, they went from Egypt to endure France's worst winter and there were no rugs for the horses. One resourceful Quartermaster Sergeant scrounged tarpaulins and cut them into horse rugs. He was punished but such was the love for their horses. Patrols had to reconnoitre enemy positions and this was fraught with danger. Often the small Light Horse patrols found that sections of the front line were deserted, so notified authorities.

In 1917, the 4th Brigade rode in support of the Australian Infantry advance on the German-held Messines Ridge. They would charge across the shell-cratered wilderness and many were killed by artillery fire. In 1918, the Germans fell back and left their machine gun posts to delay the Allied advance. Small Light Horse patrols went forward to locate them. They rode in wide scattered groups. They were fired on, they galloped to cover, swung out wide on each flank, then moved on the gun positions from both sides. The German gunners usually surrendered.

Roads were often virtually impassable and visibility often poor. The mounted troops became 'the eyes' of the rest. When the Armistice was declared on 11 November 1918, the Australian Light Horse was at the front of the allied advance. These horses faced constant danger and the vet corps worked overtime.

The vet corps treated over two and a half million animals for foot injuries, mud fever, shrapnel damage, mange and serious injuries. Most fatalities were caused by exhaustion, exposure, disease and the elements. More than twenty horse hospitals were built behind the lines.

Above: Horses take a drink, perhaps their last for two days, en route to take part in the assault on Beersheba, which took place on 31 October 1917.

Above: The 4th Light Horse Regiment en route to Beersheba.

Right: Single file and dismounted, Light Horsemen cross the mountains of Moab in what is now southern Jordan, March-April 1918.

Left: The 9th Light Horse travels along a winding road in the Judean Hills near Jerusalem in what is now Israel.

Picture: Australian War Memorial

13

What happened to the horses?

'You can't tell me that being led past dead horses and a revolver pointed at their heads, they didn't know what was about to happen.' – Henry Bostock

By the end of the war, 13,000 Australian horses remained on foreign soil. Many troopers had hoped to buy back their horses from the army but the Horse Demobilisation Committee at London's War Office issued the order that none of the horses were to return to Australia for quarantine and expense reasons. There was huge public anger and so 11,000 horses were sold to the British and Indian armies and local markets, while 2000 horses over twelve years old were to be shot. Many of these were taken to the olive groves outside Tripoli and shot by squads under the command of a veterinary officer. The men were deeply distressed.

"The day has come. I lose my horse tonight," NZ trooper Fred Sterling wrote in his diary. "[He is] the only thing in this land that I am truly sorry to leave. My very best friend in this land he has been…I love him very much."

Another soldier, Ted Andrews, one of a squad tasked with destruction of the older horses, wrote that it was the "Saddest day of the war… Each man had to hold two horses, and it was the most sickening job I had during the war. … It seemed awfully sad that these poor old faithful creatures, after suffering from thirst, hunger and fatigue and carrying heavy loads for hundreds of miles, should have to end their days by being shot down by the very people they had so faithfully served. … Some of the poor old beggars had landed here with the main body… I can tell you, it made some of us very miserable for some time afterwards, the memory of those lines of bodies lying stark in the desert, faithful unto death".[12]

12 Terry Kinloch, *Devils on Horses*, 2007, pp337-38

Goodbye my friend. An unidentified trooper, carrying saddle and bridle, says a last farewell before leaving his deceased horse.

Popular myth has it that significant numbers of troopers shot their own horses in preference to leaving them to a potentially grim fate in the Middle East, particularly those who still had their own horses they had brought with them from home. However the evidence does not support this: while some troopers did take this step, it was not widespread.

Experts have said that when the horses' bridles and saddles were removed, their manes and tails cut and shoes removed and then a revolver pointed at their heads, they knew what was about to happen. They could smell death and sense the alarm among the other horses. The carcasses were skinned and the hides salted and sold as leather to recoup some war costs. The New Zealanders, the other half of the ANZAC legend, were equally devastated when told they could not take their horses home either. 10,000 horses had been sent from New Zealand for the New Zealand Mounted Rifles.

A worse fate awaited those sold locally as beasts of burden; most of them were cruelly treated and overworked in quarries and mines. Troopers were angry, bewildered and distressed by the orders surrounding the horses as they had thought to proudly ride their horses down main streets in victory parades back home. Some soldiers could not bear the thought of their 'mates' being shot by others or sold for mine work so took them out to shoot them themselves, their closest 'cobbers'. It was considered an offence

This statue stands in Tongala, northern Victoria, a monument to the 24 Australian Light Horse regiments and their horses. The two-metre statue is of a horseman carrying an empty saddle, bridle and saddle cloth, walking away, head lowered, after saying farewell to his horse. Below the statue is the poem Farewell Old War Horse, a tribute to 120,000 Australian horses that went overseas.

Dorothy Brooke
1883-1955

Dorothy Brooke went to Egypt with her husband Major-General Geoffrey Brooke when he was posted there with the British Cavalry.

She had been devoted to horses since her childhood. She founded the Old War Horse Memorial Hospital in 1934 in Cairo – renamed the Brooke Hospital for Animals in 1961.

The Brooke charity is now one of the world's largest equine welfare organisations, at work in many countries, with headquarters in London. Her descendants retain involvement.

to shoot your horse, so many were simply recorded as missing. Grieving for their horses was acute and some struggled to recover from the ordeal of their equine friends being killed or left behind to a likely harsh fate.

"With our horses gone, our camp seemed gloomy and depressing," Colonel Olden wrote. "They had been part and parcel of our very lives all these years and now—the death sentence."

Trooper Charles Carter, a former jockey from Victoria, was one of those who destroyed his own horse. His son Ron, a former journalist, wrote in 2003 that Carter spoke often during his lifetime of his beloved horse Tim. "Before embarking from Tripoli for the trip home in mid-1919 he and his mates had to shoot their faithful four-legged friends," Ron wrote. "They could not bear the thought of their devoted mounts pulling a plough somewhere in Palestine or becoming a broken-down, ill-treated hack."[13]

Official army records did not identify or commend any horse that took part in that campaign by name. The sole identification of horses was by brand and a number engraved on the front left hoof. Banjo Paterson was heartbroken about the horses' fate and resigned from the Remount, though he was peruaded to stay a little longer. General Allenby ordered his Arabian thoroughbreds back to England for cavalry service.

Twelve years later, in 1930, Dorothy Brooke, wife of a British cavalry officer in Egypt, visited Cairo. She was a well-known socialite and an accomplished horsewoman. She had been alerted to the plight of the ex-war horses by concerned British residents in Egypt. She saw hungry, broken-down horses being beaten and expected to haul heavy loads, being slowly worked to death. She found out that they were ex-Australian, British and New Zealand horses. They had all served in WW1 and many were over twenty years old. They

13 Ron Carter *The Age* 23 November 2003

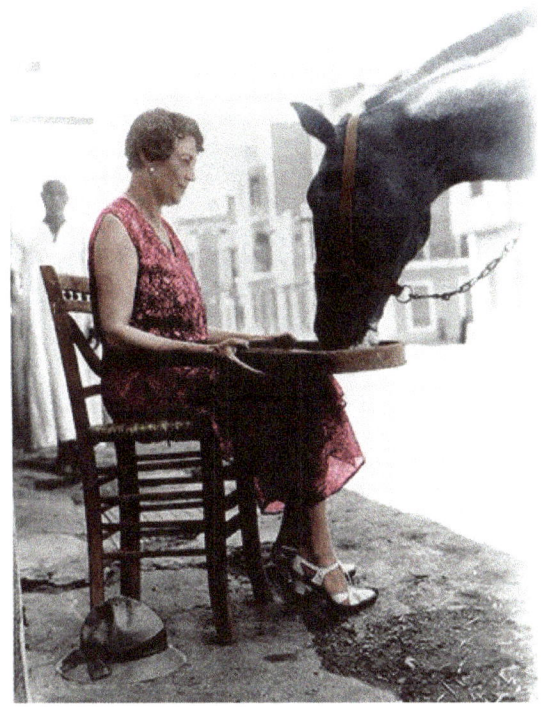 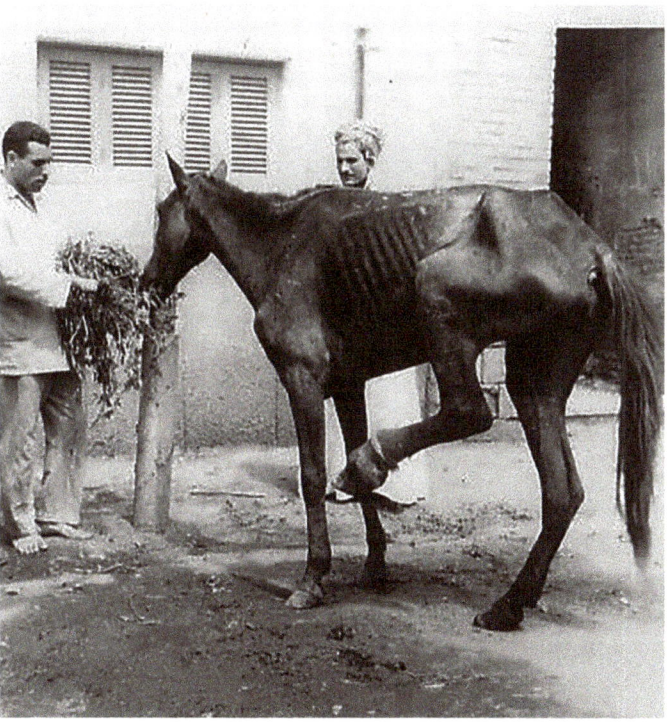

Colorised photo from the cover of one of Dorothy Brooke's books.

One of the early malnourished horses bought back from a local family by Dorothy Brooke.

had been sold by the British Army, who felt they were too costly to send home, to many poor working people in Cairo. These people themselves struggled to survive and did not have the resources to look after and feed a working horse properly. Brooke was so haunted by the horses' suffering that she started the Old War Horse Fund and raised money from the British public, friends, and also used her own funds, to buy the horses. In 1931 she wrote to the *Morning Post* newspaper in London to appeal for funds. One of her supporters was King George V.

'Old Bill,' the first former war horse Brooke saved, was elderly and lame in all four legs. She bought him in 1931 and he was humanely euthanased. She made a promise that she would find his equine comrades from the Great War and liberate them; she found over 200 at first, and between 1930 and 1934 she bought back and returned 5000 old war horses to Britain.

"Happiness comes like a dream of the past to these old horses when we buy them," she wrote in her diary in 1932. "They cock their ears at an English voice, they even whinny with the old familiar smell of bran mash … As their ill-shod misshapen hooves felt the deep tibbin [barley straw] bed beneath them, there would be another doubting, disbelieving, halt. Then gradually they would lower their heads and sniff as though they could not believe their own eyes or noses. Memories, long forgotten, would then return when some stepped eagerly forwards towards the mangers piled high with berseem [a type of clover], while others, with creaking joints, lowered themselves slowly on the bed and lay, necks and legs outstretched. There they remained flat out, until hand fed."

Brooke never blamed the people in Egypt who, through poverty and lack of knowledge, had not looked after the horses properly. With this insight she saw the need to set up a free animal hospital in Cairo, so that every poor owner could bring his horse, which could be the family's sole means of earning a living, and get help and advice at the first signs of trouble. And so the Brooke Animal Hospital was built. What foresight, compassion and understanding, to offer prevention and education rather than punishment and judgement.

Her compassion and understanding of the amazing feats that these old war horses had undergone is heartening. She knew that the horses had already had a hard life. They had carried too much weight, experienced rationing, withstood piercing cold, dust and exhaustion, suffered both severe and light wounds, covered great distances, suffered the severe heat of the Jordan Valley and, most heart wrenching, being separated from their constant companions and friends, the troopers with whom they had formed an immense bond of love and interdependence.

Each retrieved horse was given rest and loving care, finally receiving the respect due to them. However many had to be humanely put out of their misery.

In 1934, Brooke set up the permanent Old War Horse Memorial Hospital in Cairo. It cared for the surviving war horses and other working horses in the city. The Brooke, as it is now called, is an international horse welfare charity.

At the end of the war...

Bill the Bastard survived and remained at Gallipoli helping collect and transport the belongings of dead soldiers and other bits and pieces left behind. It is believed he was sold to a Turkish farmer at Gallipoli and lived out his life. He died in 1924 and was buried near the main grave site and was given a headstone. A rare honour for a brave war horse.

Plain Bill and Bally, the mounts of Ryrie and Chauvel, were sent to England.

Sandy, General Bridges' horse, was sent back to Australia and turned out to graze at the Central Remount Depot at Maribyrnong. Due to increasing blindness and debility, he was humanely put down in May 1923.

Bess, General Powles horse from New Zealand, was sent home in 1920 and died there in 1934.

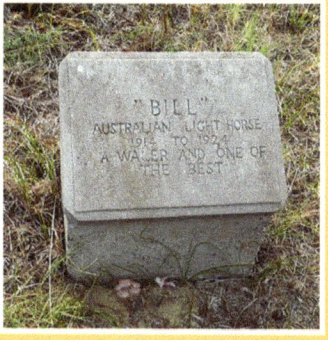

Memorial at the burial site of Bill the Bastard, in the shadow of Walker's Ridge, Gallipoli.
It reads:

"Bill"
Australian Light Horse
1914 – 1924
A Waler and one of the best"

General Harry Chauvel on his charger,
Damascus, Syria, 21 October 1918.
Photograph by Lt James Pinkerton Campbell

Farewell Old War Horse

This poem by an unknown author was inspired by the feelings of the Lighthorsemen, who had to leave their horses in the Middle East on their return to Australia.

The struggle for freedom has ended they say
The days of fatigue and remorse
But our hearts one and all are in memory today
We are losing our old friend, the Horse.

The old quadruped that has carried us thro'
The sand ridden caravan track
And shared in the charge of the gallant and true
With the boys who will never come back.

Oh those long weary days thro' a miniature hell
Short of water and nothing to eat
Each hour we climbed down for a few minutes' spell
And dozed safe and sound at your feet.

When the enemy shrapnel broke overhead
As we passed up that Valley of Death
You never once slackened in the hail of lead
Through the boldest of all held their breath.

But we never forget you, old comrade and friend
When the QM Dump hove in sight
What the Buckshee to Gippos we scored in the end
And your rations were double that night.

Then came the long journey, the greatest of all
The cavalry stunt of the world
The sons of Australia had answered the call
And the Ensign of Freedom unfurled.

And now we are leaving you footsore and worn
To the land where the Mitchell grass grew
Where you frolicked like lambs in the sweet scented morn
To the song of the Dismal Curlew.

So farewell to the Yarraman old warhorse, farewell
Be you mulga bred chestnut or bay
If there's a hereafter for horses as well
Then may we be with you some day.

14

Conclusion

'As I write, I can hear the horses gallop, the ground shaking under their hooves, going on to win a bloody and drawn-out war...'

In all official presentations regarding WW1 the role of the horses has been understated, and the order that no horses were to return to Australia undermined their important role. They were not treated with the respect that a soldier deserved. One can only applaud General Sir William Bridges, the first Commander in Chief of the Australian Imperial Forces, who was killed at Gallipoli, who ordered that his warhorse, Sandy, his companion and mate, be returned to Australia. Sandy is the only horse that made it home. He walked down Collins Street for the State funeral procession for General Bridges. He was a reminder, testament to the great bond forged between man and horse in one of the most brutal conflicts in Australia's history.

Similarly, Colonel Powles of the New Zealand Mounted Rifles was passionate about his war horse, Bess, who was with him right through the Desert Campaign, and ensured that she, and three other mounts, returned to New Zealand. She was sent to England for quarantine and took part in the victory parade in Berlin. When she died later at a good age, she was buried on a hill in New Zealand with a modest gravestone.

Luckily for some horses, they led useful and cared-for lives. At the end of the war, many horsess were shipped to England for army use. Two geldings—Bally, Chauvel's horse, and Plain Bill, General Ryrie's horse—were sent as remounts for the standing army. They were ridden in many fox hunts in England and enjoyed good retirements.

For the Light Horseman, his horse was an "extension of himself" and deserved the honour and treatment that a returned soldier deserved. Sandy is buried somewhere in a paddock not far from the remount headquarters at Maribyrnong and hopefully a monument can be erected to acknowledge a man's love for his beloved horse. A group of Maribyrnong residents have run a 'Friends of Sandy" campaign since 2000 to see a fitting memorial for Sandy created on the hill. This was officially recognised on October 30, 2017, with the unveiling of the Sandy Memorial to all the horses that did not return. The permanent memorial will eventually be located on a site in front of the Fisher Stables at the remount yard in Maribyrnong.

In May 2023, a statue of Sandy was unveiled in Tallangatta, his birthplace.

At the end of the war, General Allenby, (British) wrote a remarkable tribute to the Light Horsemen: "The Australian Light Horseman combines a splendid physique and a restless activity of mind. This mental quality renders him somewhat impatient of rigid and formal discipline, but it confers upon him the gift of adaptability, and this is the secret of much of his success mounted or on foot. In this dual role... the Australian Light Horse man has proved himself equal to the best... he has earned the gratitude of the Empire and the admiration of the world."

This a fitting recognition of the Australian soldier's ability, 'their laid back, laconic style yet fierce battle ability to stand against superior forces'. But how can he only acknowledge the role of the riders? The horses should be included in any tribute because it was together that the horses and riders were able to succeed in the campaign. A fitting tribute might read: "The Australian horseman and his horse proved equal to the best... they have earned the gratitude of the empire and the admiration of the world."

It is recognition of an astute and careful Australian leader, Harry Chauvel, a brilliant horseman, that he was the only Australian given the responsibility of controlling a cavalry corps in the British Army. Chauvel praised his soldiers for their intelligence and extraordinary humour in all circumstances in a speech made after his arrival back in Melbourne.

Chauvel recognised that the race meetings and mounted games that were held during the desert campaign were essential events to boost the morale of battle-weary troopers. At races staged at Rafa in March 1917, two months after the battle, Chauvel commented, "we have had a great day, today... the course was lovely—right in the middle of the battlefield of Rafa!" His division won five out of six races and "my own horse, Bally, ran third in the steeplechase."

These racing and sports events during wartime also included the mounted tug-of-war, wrestling on horseback and jumping events. They had to improvise a lot of the time. One thing that Chauvel insisted on was his principle that 'The rider should always think of his mount before himself.' It is testament to the man's love for his horses, especially when he had to leave Bally behind, that when he returned to Melbourne his horse Digger was brought to his house each morning and he rode around the Tan!*

He later learned that his magnificent bay gelding had been sent to England at the end of the war for the standing army. Bally won the 'handy jump' at army championships held at Aldershot, England, in 1919.

Banjo Paterson was always concerned for the welfare of the horses. His work at the remount depots is a credit to him and his team. When he was told about the fate of the horses from the Horse Demobilisation Committee in the War Office he commented, "How would those bloody grey Pommie bureaucrats understand anything about the bonds between the troopers and their mounts." In November 1918, Paterson and Aidan Sutherland led 128 horses into the desert and met the captain of the machine-gun squadron. Paterson said he felt like a mass murderer and could not watch the destruction of the horses.

Unfortunately, the English sense of propriety in times past and a belief in the superiority of their thoroughbred horses perhaps explains why they viewed the Australian Waler horses as "a common, hairy-legged lot...with poor breeding". Yet these horses proved themselves over the five years to be adaptable, durable, and able to withstand the harsh conditions in the desert. From the daring charge at Beersheba to the Long March to Damascus, they were instrumental in enabling the British empire to win the war. They proved to be the best horses in desert warfare. They should have received the same honours as their riders, who would attest to the great bond they had with their horses, their 'mates' who faced it all with them. It is a tragedy they were not honoured and given the right to return home and recover, spending their last days in the shade enjoying retirement, but were instead rewarded with death or ending their days in hard work on foreign soil.

Research published in 2013 in the journal *Social Anthropology* found that riders and horses can enter into a unique state of 'interspecies', of co-being, with one another. Each partner evolves to 'fit' better with the other, both physically and mentally. "As riders get to know their horses, they attune to them—they learn both mental and physical ways of acting...You cannot view them individually but as one, unique combined notion," the article said.[14]

On a visit to the Australian Light Horse Memorial Park in Seymour, Victoria, I was

---

* The Tan – walking track around the Botanic Gardens in Melbourne.

struck by a moving confession about how much the horses meant to some soldiers.

"The only person I could talk to about things that I really cared about—my family, my mum and my fear of dying—was my horse. And I'd go to my horse at night and I'd feed him and I'd stand there, and I'd stroke his neck and talk into his ear and I'd tell him...and that horse listened." The inscription on the plaque was confided to Michael Morpugo by a WW1 veteran, and recorded in *The Diggers Menagerie* by Barry Stone.

The New Zealand Mounted Rifles troopers loved their horses as the Australians did. "The patient endurance of toil and pain by the horses was constantly a source of wonder to the men, and made almost a human bond between horse and rider," noted the *Official War History of the NZ Mounted Rifles Regiment 1914-19*.[15]

In this narrative I have attempted to reveal that the horses of the Australian Light Horse regiments did have names and personalities and will be remembered for their undying loyalty and bravery. It is not easy to find the words from the soldiers to show this interdependence, but enough actions are noted, poems written, and general recognition is available to confirm the bond that existed. Troopers generally tried to keep letters home upbeat, and also for the horsemen it would not have been easy recording personal thoughts as they were always on the move, on horseback, riding all night and when they stopped, they slept.

I have included photographs, paintings and poems that are moving and capture the special bond between horse and man. I have also included tributes and a list of memorials which cannot fail to stir one's emotions. If you read Tennyson's six-stanza poem *The Charge of the Light Brigade* and realise the significance of the horror faced by horse and man in this historic moment, you will notice that it is not until the fifth stanza that the horses are mentioned. In contrast, Eric Bogle's haunting ballad, *As If He Knows* depicts the pain of the horses, and the ingratitude of a nation is etched in the last line,

> "and all that we've been through
> A nation's gratitude
> Was a dusty grave."

There is a photo in various WW1 archives which highlights the horrific conditions man

---

14 Anita Maurstad, PhD, University of Tromsø, Norway, 'Co-being and intra-action in horse–human relationships', *Social Anthropology*, August 2013.
15 Official War History of the NZ Mounted Rifles Regiment 1914-19, p243

created in the First World War. It is of German horses wearing gas masks on the Western Front in 1917. It was taken during the longest battle and on one day, 7000 horses were killed by shelling.

But to counterbalance this image a little, there is the beautiful painting by Australian military artist, Ron Marshall, called 'Sharing his water' which captures the special moment between an exhausted and thirsty digger and his mount, sharing water from his hat. This was not an unusual occurrence. I think that that image says it all.

"Most obediently and often most painfully they died — faithful unto death."

15
Tributes to the horses

A collection of tributes across the years to the Walers of the Light Horse

1. John Moore – "Wherever man has left his footprint in the long ascent from barbarism to civilisation we will find the hoof print of the horse beside it."

2. Sgt Barry 'Bow' Legg – "These fine old comrades had carried us faithfully under all sorts of hardships: through long marches in deep Sinai sand; through the steep and rocky Judean Hills. And then perhaps the hardest of all, in those long, exhausting treks across the Jordan and up the goat tracks of the mountains of Moab, … often going without water for nearly two days at a time."

3. Major Oliver Hogue ('Trooper Bluegum') excerpt from *The Horses Stayed Behind*, a poem.

Major Oliver Hogue wrote as 'Trooper Bluegum'

"I don't think I could stand the thought
Of my old fancy hack
Just crawling round old Cairo with a
Gyppo on his back.
Perhaps some English tourist out in
Palestine may find
My broken-hearted Waler with a
Wooden plough behind."

4. JM Brereton, *The Horse in War* – "On campaign, riding and tending the same horse for months on end, sleeping in the open only a few yards behind the picket-lines at night, and suffering the same privations, the soldier came to regard his horse almost as an extension of his own being."

5. AB (Banjo) Paterson – "a mate through suffering and deprivation; a bond developed between man and beast, a feeling of affection and trust—a real partnership."

6. AB Banjo Paterson – poem, *The Last Parade*.

7. Memorial – "Most obediently and often most painfully they died—faithful unto death." Inscription on memorial at St Jude on the Hill in Hampstead, UK, erected in honour of horses killed during the First World War.

8. Jill, Duchess of Hamilton – Referring to a photo in her first book, she writes: "In the photo, the horse is as important as the rider. Take away the horse and the picture means nothing. The animal gives potency to the rider." And in writing of her father, Noel 'Robbie' Robertson, she says – "his horse carried him through the Desert Campaign and rather than sell him to harsh treatment, he rode his horse for one last gallop, dismounted and tied a handkerchief onto the horse's bridle to shield its eyes and shot him. He shot his companion that he loved and trusted. He killed part of himself."

9. Poem, unknown author –
   In the fading memory of tears and terror
   Does our nation remember its mortal error?
   A thousand more and a thousand more
   A breed of horses went to war.
   From NSW we mustered them all
   For king and country to rise and fall,
   They carried us; wearied, bloodied and dry,
   Never a query or what for? Or why?
   We sheltered beneath their salt crusted hides.
   They trusted our voices, laid down and died.
   Those that were left
   Became dust on the shore
   Lest we forget
   The perils of War.

10. Barry Rogers, Light Horseman – "well, basically, the horse was your mate."

11. Major Chaplain William Devine – "The bond was absolute. The men fretted over the welfare of their horses, especially when water was scarce." Chaplain Devine was speaking at a welcome home celebration held at Gisborne Mechanics Hall, Victoria, on 19 August 1919. Devine had been assigned to a unit and got to know the horsemen over four years. He remembered his unit being ordered far out into the desert. They went 105 miles (170km) by train. All rode in open trucks, the horses having the best of it. Then the horses were pulled out and the regiment started on a trek of six days across the desert to their first camp. No rations except what each man carried, no tents, no cookers, no billy to boil water. Riding all day in a blazing sun, lying in the frosty nights at their horses' heads. On the fifth day the water ran out, and that evening when horses and men were at the last gasp with exhaustion and thirst, he saw 'Australian soldiers emptying their water bottles into their hats to give their poor horse a drink….'

12. Guy Powles, NZ Mounted Rifles – "We New Zealanders are all horse lovers by our British birthright, and as colonials, we have learnt to value the horse as a means of existence. They learnt that to no man is a horse so essential as to the mounted soldier. His horse is more than a friend, he is part of the soldier's very life."

13. Edwin McKay, NZ – "When the gruelling test came later in the Sinai and Palestine, we loved our horses with a feeling that went deeply into our beings. They were more than mounts to shift us from spot to spot, they were cobbers."

14. Hector Dinning, Australian war correspondent – "What stood out was that these men were modest and unsophisticated, loved their horses, were careless of danger and felt it was important their horses have water, food and grooming."

15. Anecdote, unknown author – There was a lack of water in the desert and an old pack horse, smelling the water, struggled to his feet and staggered up to the group. "Shout the old chap a pint," said a trooper.

16. Alec McNeur, NZ Mounted Rifles – "Those wonderful NZ horses, how they toiled to move us. They could always be depended upon."

17. Unknown author – "There they were, lying dead in rows and not given the decent burial they so richly deserved. Many of them had more battle scars than the men who rode them." (A comment made about the shooting of the horses.)

18. Song dedicated to the Walers:
As If He Knows, Eric Bogle, July 2001
It's as if he knows
He's standing close to me
His breath warm on my sleeve
His head hung low
It's as if he knows
What the dawn will bring
The end of everything
For my old Banjo
And all along the picket lines beneath the desert sky
The Light Horsemen move amongst their mates to say one last goodbye
And the horses stand so quietly
Row on silent row
It's as if they know

Time after time
We rode through shot and shell
We rode in and out of Hell
On their strong backs
Time after time
They brought us safely through
By their swift sure hooves
And their brave hearts
Tomorrow we will form up ranks and march down to the quay
And sail back to our loved ones in that dear land across the sea
While our loyal and true companions
Who asked so little and gave so much
Will lie dead in the dust.

For the orders came
No horses to return
We were to abandon them
To be slaves

After all we'd shared
And all that we'd been through
A nation's gratitude
Was a dusty grave

For we can't leave them to the people here, we'd rather see them dead
So each man will take his best mate's horse with a bullet through the head
For the people are like their land
Wild and cruel and hard
So Banjo, here's your reward.

19. Major Walter Urquhart, Staff Officer attached to General Chauvel, noting the love that troopers felt for their horses – "On patrol, saw a lone trooper with his horse down, exhausted from heat and lack of water had emptied his own water bottle into a canvas bucket. Chauvel dismounted and emptied his water bottle into the bucket and expected the others to do the same."

20. Henry Gullett, 'The Horses Stay Behind', *Kia Ora Coo-ee* magazine, November 1918 – "Among the troopers you find hundreds of horses, less pleasing, perhaps, to the eye, but equally spirited and equally hard to kill…The horses we have ridden will always stand first in our affections."

21. Anon – 'Our Army Horses', *Kia Ora Coo-ee*, June 1918 – "Horses and riders achieved something that should cause an extra laurel wreath to be hung on the memorial of Anzac victories. How often have we turned out with our faithful animals, already weary after many hours riding, and galloped off to attack some strong Turkish position miles away."

22. "Acrabah" (pen name) – 'Mulga', *Kia Ora Coo-ee*, December 1918 – A tribute to the horse Mulga, owned by big Jim Morton, who was killed in the advance on Damascus: "Many a night, with the column creeping like some monstrous, evil serpent through the darkness, Mulga picked his way through the treacherous boulders and wadi beds with light-footed precision, while for hours his rider slept a swaying, dreamless sleep in the saddle."

23. H. Spence, 'Pal o' Mine', *Kia Ora Coo-ee*, May 1918 – A story which speaks of the death of a horse at Beersheba – "On lonely patrol or nerve-trying night screen you

were company, and ears and eyes to me – aye – and shield to me, too."
The story mentions a connection between his 'spirit' and that of his horse. It is an incredibly moving piece.

24. Letter from Bill Griffiths, age 85, from Mansfield, recalls his father's experiences in the Desert Campaign and is full of praise for the horses.

25. 'Light Horse Anthem' by 'Bitten', Palestine, 1918. (Written on a scrap of paper picked up on the Jordan-Jerusalem road; Printed in Kia Ora Coo-ee, October 1918:

We are the mobile forces,
The Desert Mountain Corps;
We roam around the country
In search of Turkish gore,
In every kind of weather,
In heat or dust or damp;
But every time we settle down
They shift the blooming camp!

We dig the winding trenches'
As well as groom the horse,
Mid Jordan's heat and dust clouds
And Auja's swampy course.
Yet when we go to Bethl'hem
To easy up the strain,
Somebody gives the order, and off we go again!

Sometimes we ask for transport
To shift some extra kit;
The answer is, 'You're mobile,'
Or 'You should not have it,'
Yet when we form a small dump
Way down along the line
Some irate 'red – tab' fellow
Kicks up a blinkin' shine!

And so we keep on moving
As days and weeks roll by;
The records of our movements
The Turkish staff Defy.
And when we get to Berlin
The Kaiser he will say:
'Hoch! Hoch! Mein Gott! They cannot
At last have found the way.

26. Neil Andrew's poem, *I Spoke To You In Whispers*, demonstrates an understanding of how the soldiers felt the pain their horses could be suffering in battle:

I spoke to you in whispers
As shells made the ground beneath us quake
We both trembled in that crater
A toxic muddy bloody lake
I spoke to you and pulled your ears
To try to quell your fearful eye
As bullets whizzed through the raindrops
And we watched the men around us die
I spoke to you in stable tones
A quiet tranquil voice
At least I volunteered to fight
You didn't get to make the choice
I spoke to you of old times
Perhaps you went before the plough
And pulled the hay cart from the meadow
Far from where we're dying now
I spoke to you of grooming
Of when the ploughman made you shine
Not the shrapnel wounds and bleeding flanks
Mane filled with mud and wire and grime
I spoke to you of courage
As gas filled the Flanders air
Watched you struggle in the mud
Harness acting like a snare
I spoke to you of promises

If from this maelstrom I survive
By pen and prose and poetry
I'll keep your sacrifice alive
I spoke to you of legacy
For when this hellish time is through
All those who hauled or charged or carried
Will be regarded heroes too
I spoke to you in dulcet tones
Your eye told me you understood
As I squeezed my trigger to bring you peace
The only way I could
And I spoke to you in whispers.

I Spoke To You In Whispers is generally reproduced accompanied by a painting of a soldier comforting a dying horse on the road in WW1.

27. Edwin Charles Douglas Husband, 'A Waler's Story', 1919 – An account by 'Baldy' (a horse) of conditions in the desert campaign. From *Australia in Palestine*, edited by war historian Henry Gullett et al.

28. Anon, 'Our Army Horses' in the *Kia Ora Coo-ee*, June 1918, expresses this sentiment: "To these animals is due much of the credit for the manner in which the enemy was pursued, and the broken remnants of the Ottoman Empire were pushed further towards Constantinople. Horses and riders achieved something that should cause an extra laurel wreath to be hung on the memorial of Anzac victories."

29. Lord Mottistone (General Jack Seely) – "In the first words of my book [*Warrior: The Amazing Story of a Real War Horse*] I have told of my conviction that man and horse are an inseparable unit." His horse, Warrior, was with him throughout the campaign on the Western Front. "By his supreme courage at a critical moment, he led me forward to victory in perhaps the greatest crisis of the war."

30. Winston Churchill, a life-long equestrian, could not abandon the loyal war horses at the end of WW1. He saved tens of thousands after he learnt that the horses were at risk of disease, hunger and death at the hands of French and Belgian butchers because he could not get them back to British soil. He was so angry that on 13 February 1919, he wrote to Lt-General Sir Travers Clarke, (Quartermaster-general at the time.) Due to Churchill's intervention, extra vessels were sent to collect the horses – 9000 per week. In the end, 62,000 horses were returned to England.

While this is admirable, it is a shame that the same was not done for the Australian and New Zealand horses.

31. Elyne Mitchell, daughter of sir Harry Chauvel – "In the management of the horses, and the complete dependence of each horse on its owner for water, food, attention, strengthened the bond between man and horse."

32. Trooper and author Ion Idriess speaks of men almost crying over wounded and dead horses because "we love our horses."

33. *The Anzac on the Wall*, a poem by Jim Brown about the extraordinary bond between man and horse.

34. Poem. *The Horse That Died For Me* by Edwin 'Trooper Gerardy' Gerard –
.... I urged my horse with a purpose grim for a ridge where
   Cover lay,
And my heart beat high for the heart of him when he saved
   My life that day.
His knees gave way and I slipped from him; he dropped in
   A sprawling heap
On the wind-gapped edge of the skyline's rim where the
   High- blown sand was deep.
And fear came down with a gusty rain of lead on his final
   Bed...

Before I turned for cover again, I knew that his life had fled.
My heart is warm for a heart that died in the desert flank
    Attack,
And the white sand surges down to hide and bones of a
    Faithful trooper's hack.

35. *The Horses Stay Behind (One Last Ride)* This song written by Kerrie Gambley of the family band Haystack Mountain Hermits was inspired by her great-grandfather, a Gallipoli veteran who on his deathbed shared his terrible sadness at leaving his horse Ebenezer in Palestine when he sailed for home. The heart-wrenching song was reimagined as a music video in preparation for Anzac Day 2023. Twenty Australian Light Horse members travelled to Queensland and saddled up for dawn and sunset film shoots in the Tamborine Mountain area in Queensland. Australian Light Horse president, Lawrence Watts, said the words of the song struck an immediate chord with his members.

"I think it will also resonate with the wider community because a lot of people have a very personal relationship with their horse, based on trust," he said.

GOING TO JERICHO.

"Go to Jericho". One often hears that expression, but how many who use it know what a journey through the wilderness to Jericho really means? With a woman friend, I once made the jaunt, and here is my traveller's tale.

Down in the fertile plains of Jericho, a very interesting tribe lives, and pastures numerous flocks and herds on land that was once covered by the suburbs of the great cities of Sodom and Gomorrah. The Dead Sea now covers these biblical "Cities of the plain". We were warned before starting not to go through the "Valley of Robbers", which lies between Bethlehem and the Dead Sea, but we were not afraid of these "robbers", inasmuch as we must have been personally acquainted with several. Our first afternoon's journey, three hours out from Bethlehem, brought us to Mar Saba, or Saint Saba, in the heart of this biblical wilderness, where dwelt a small company of monks. Their abode was not a monastery, but a group of tiny one-room cells, scattered about just anywhere, the whole lot enclosed by a wall. Nothing female is ever allowed to enter this monastery's enclosure, therefore, we had to spend the night in a tower outside, where Russian women pilgrims were in the habit of staying. Just one lonely old Greek priest kept this ancient tower, the entrance to which was an opening high up in the side. A long ladder led up to it.

The priest of the tower warned us very urgently against taking the route through the "Valley of Robbers," but we were willing to risk an attack by "our friends", the Arabs, especially as we carried nothing that was worth stealing, and so pursued our way, starting at about 5 a.m. We carried no money with us, the donkey boy had a few piastres with which to buy barley for the donkey, and that was all. We had been riding only about two hours when we beheld a large company of people coming from another direction, also towards the dread Valley. Eighty or ninety stalwart Bedawin composed the party. They no sooner came near enough to recognise us than we were overcome with joyful greetings and salutations. It was a body of men of the Ta-ameri tribe, old friends of ours, on their way to Amman, to build the Mecca railroad. They inquired by which road we were going; it proved to be their route as well, and we had an impregnable escort right through the dangerous Valley down to the Dead Sea.

When safely out of the Valley, we sat down and had breakfast with our Arab friends, for they would not leave us until we were beyond the dangerous district. We rode past a place called Nebbi Mousa, supposed by the people there to be the spot where Moses was buried, and so came to the Dead Sea in the late afternoon. Nebbi Mousa is a shrine, and the scene of many pilgrimages. Once a year, at about Easter time, crowds of people from Jerusalem, Hebron, Nablus, and neighbouring villages ride down on camels to this place. They are led by Dervishes, who perform ghastly religious acts of self torture, drive skewers through their cheeks, cut themselves with knives, and often throw themselves on the ground, to be walked over by the horses and camels, all the time calling on Allah, Mohammed and Moses. But we went on our peaceful way that time, undisturbed by such scenes, and next day reached the Arab tribes camped outside Jericho. I was at once asked to go and see a sick boy, the only son of his widowed mother. The boy had fever, so I prepared a dose of the old time fever mixture; but it was only after much argument and explanation that the mother, begging and praying me not to kill her boy, let me give him the dose. That afternoon we went to St. John's Monastery, situated on the banks of the Jordan. This was a Greek Monastery, with only one monk on the premises.

During the day we spent our time down on the banks of the Jordan, where the people used to come to us with their ailments and troubles, but night always found us back at the convent, a little further up the hill-side. There was a certain place at the Jordan where baptisms took place, and near it, a small Greek steamer lay anchored, awaiting permission from Constantinople to ply up and down the river, and on the Dead Sea. It had waited for many months, and seemed likely to wait for many more. In the meantime, the Captain of the ship, a stalwart man, made himself useful to the Greek priests by assisting them with their multitudinous baptisms of Russian Pilgrims of "ripe years", at Eastertide. The priests were not very strong, so they read the service while the Captain did the dipping. Each pilgrim retired into the thick bushes that flanked the river, disrobed, and reappeared attired in one long white garment. Three times had each individual to be dipped. The sturdy Captain held them firmly by the shoulders, and down each one went out of sight under the flowing waves. The shrieks and ejaculations, the wild splutterings and struggles for breath as each dripping figure was lifted out—only to be dipped in again — can be imagined.

When, at last, our Jordan visit was over, and we were preparing to leave for home, a shepherd boy came up, and asked if we were the people who had visited the camp at Jericho a few days before, and given a sick boy medicine. "Yes", we said, "how is he?" "Perfectly well" answered the boy. "His mother prays for you all the time, and everybody in the camp wants you to come back and give them all some of that medicine". Here was a predicament. However, back we had to go. As we neared the camp they crowded out to meet us, and we were practically mobbed by a shouting, jostling, but good natured mob, begging us for some of the marvellous medicine. We asked why they wanted medicine when they were all perfectly well. They said: "We may get ill, and you've never been here before, and may never come again, so what's to happen to us? We'll take your medicine as a precaution".

We dismounted, and divided all our little store of household remedies into doses for everybody. In a few moments, however, it became impossible to work, for the crowds were making a terrible row. We told them that they must keep quiet. The men said they would settle things for us; it was the women who were making all the noise. They provided themselves with sticks, and rushed about flourishing them over the women's heads, shouting to them to "shut up", and incidentally making far more noise than ever the women had made. It was a jovial Bedlam for a while, until the native woman, my companion, started telling them stories. The effect was miraculous, and thenceforward quiet reigned. We had Epsom salts, quinine, arrowroot, and such like remedies. The arrowroot we gave to the children, and the rest was distributed among the adults indiscriminately. Everywhere we went, after that, we were followed by somebody asking for medecine, or plasters for sores.

Cairo.   M.B. Mc. CONAGHY.

PAL O' MINE.

I chose you, not for symmetry of form, beauty or well-bred looks (you had none of these), but for the brand you bore, K.Y. under bar K.Y., sure in the knowledge that you would carry me well, you desert-bred son of a desert-bred dam.

Light you made of the endless miles of loose sand and the whaleback dunes of Sinai, for there are wide areas of "sand" country in that north west corner of New South Wales whence you came. But what of the shade and perfume of golden-blossomed mulga, the silver-leafed boree and pungent-scented Gnelia? What of the tree-fringed lakes, blue as the summer sky, that came into view when you raced to the top of some pine-capped sandhill, and stood at gaze, your mane and tail flowing in the wind? Was it in search of these that, with ears pricked, you eagerly topped those dunes of Sinai? And was it of regret, that sigh which vibrated your velvet nostrils when you saw only burning sand? I believe so.

Were the journey never so long, and the fodder and water never so short, you would still carry me "on the bib"; distance, drought and days between drinks were your heritage. On lonely patrol or nerve-trying night screen you were company, and ears and eyes to me — aye, and shield to me, too. That night, when we were feeling our way ahead, I seeing nought, you, nosing the air, tense and alert, suddenly swerved and leaped aside just as a spurt of flame stabbed the darkness, and a bullet's breath fanned my cheek.

To the sound of grimmer plaudits than were wont to greet your forefathers, your last race was run, and the goal was reached, Pal O' Mine. Your exile was worth the while for that glorious charge on Beersheba. With foam-flecked lips and ears laid flat, you strained to be in the van; and just when it seemed that your patron saint, or mine, was working overtime—"plunk", and with a sob, you pitched and went "West." Mercifully swift the end, for which I commended some Turk's soul to Allah.

Your spirit is surely in that Happy Hunting Ground of Honest Horses, where drought, heat, and "regulation scale for light mobile" are unknown. When I, too, go "West", my spirit shall go on pilgrimage to the Mecca of Loyal Friends; it will cross over the hills of the Mountain-bred, and the treeless haunt of the Plain-bred to a scrub-fringed sandhill whose base is aflame with Desert Pea blossoms, there to call to your spirit, Pal o' Mine.

Egypt.   H. SPENCE.

OUR ROYAL (HORSE) 'AIR SERVICE: A SPINNING NOSE DIVE.

16

Some horses mentioned

1. Midnight – Lt. Guy Haydon could not bear to be separated from his mare, a champion racehorse, Midnight. She was born at midnight, 31 October 1905, at Bloomfield Stud in the Hunter Valley in NSW. She was a magnificent black stockhorse with a three-pointed white star like a tiara on her head. When training in the desert, she won the sprint race, flag race and equitation test. Haydon, after returning to camp from Gallipoli, left no stone unturned to find his horse, which carried him through the Desert Campaign, until she was shot in the belly as she flew over a Turkish trench at Beersheba and died. The date, 31 October 1918, was 13 years to the day and date since Midnight was born.

Taffy after a good roll in the sand.

2. Taffy – Corporal Austin Edwards loved his horse, Taffy. Edwards was seriously wounded at the Battle of Romani and Taffy stood still in the thick of battle and waited for his wounded rider to mount him and race to safety. Taffy did this on the tumultuous and deafening battlefield where all his instincts were would have been telling him to flee from the noise and terror, but love and loyalty overrode this.

3. Sandy – Major-General Sir William Bridges stayed with his horse, Sandy, a big bay, on the ship to Egypt when he contracted pneumonia. He stayed with the other horses also, and was often seen beneath deck spending time with the horses. Just before his

death, Bridges gave orders that his beloved chestnut thoroughbred be sent home to Australia. Sandy was the only horse to return home.

4. Warrior – General Jack Seely and his horse Warrior were well known on the Western Front. Warrior was a courageous and brave horse who survived many near-death experiences and in an obituary published on his death in 1941 was dubbed, "the horse the Germans could not kill." Warrior lived to the ripe old age of 32.

5. Trooper Noel 'Robbie' Robertson of the 10th Light Horse would become overcome with emotion at his daughter's mention of his horse, who was with him throughout the Desert Campaign. He shot him at the end of the war and rarely spoke of him after he returned home.

6. Harry Bostock's horse helped itself to the Christmas feast by eating all Harry's bread and biscuits.

7. 'Galloping' Jack Royston. A photo shows that while he sat outside his tent, his charger was drinking out of his cup of tea.

8. Paddy – Sergeant George Auchterlonie of 8th Light Horse Regiment, Victoria, arrived in Egypt with Paddy in 1915. They went through everything together. His horse was classified c.1.1 on 27 January 1919 and was shot in the mass grave behind the camp in Tripoli.

9. 'Bill the Bastard' – Major Michael Shanahan befriended Bill, a huge chestnut with spirit, intelligence, durability and strength. He always bucked when asked to gallop. He carried five men—three on his back and one on each stirrup—for more than a kilometre during the Battle of Romani in 1916. He dashed through soft sand at a lumbering gallop without bucking to escape attacking Turks. He showed great bravery, loyalty and endurance. He carried the wounded Shanahan to safety and was rewarded with other duties after Shanahan could no longer ride him in active duty. At the end of the war, he was sold to a Turkish peasant farmer near Suvla to escape the fate of other horses. He died in 1924 and was honoured with a headstone-topped grave.

10. Tom – Colonel John Monash had a gentle and well-mannered horse called Tom who was strong, willing and responsive.

11. Babanooka – Colonel Thomas Todd had a horse called Babanooka who was the best-handicapped horse in Egypt and was used in races when training.

12. Flame – Belonged to a New Zealand trooper. Flame stayed with her wounded master, even when snipers were shooting. She dragged him to safety.

13. Bess – Colonel Guy Powles, NZ Mounted Rifles, had his horse, Bess, throughout the Desert Campaign. He sent her to England for quarantine at the end of the war and rode her in the Victory Parade in Berlin. She returned to New Zealand and lived out her life until her death at age 34.

The one-eyed war horse Nelson.

14. Nelson – Alfred Henn, an English cavalry rider, had a one-eyed war horse called Nelson. The horse was unflinching in dangerous situations and had an uncanny sense of danger. He was ridden with the full weight of a gun carriage behind him and galloped directly into gunfire that was cutting down foot soldiers. The pair had an incredible bond. They "shared terror—forged a bond—slept together in the mud to ward off the cold." Henn kept a photo of his war horse that he treasured until he died at age 101.

15. Nutty – Tasmanian John 'Jack' Hutton, 17th Battalion, wrote a tribute to Nutty, a chestnut gelding. "I was his groom and the comradeship between us was well-nigh unbelievable. His happy disposition won him popularity with the troops and even after many years he remains in their minds…In many ways he was almost human and among all the four-footed friends who served us so faithfully and well, he was without peer."

16. Plain Bill – Brigadier-General Granville de Laure Ryrie, leader of the 2nd Light Horse Brigade in Anzac Division, had a favourite horse, a thoroughbred called Plain Bill. He was devastated to leave Plain Bill and did not know what happened to him. A few years after the war an anonymous poem was published—it could perhaps have been by Ryrie.

To Bill

Plain Bill, you are wanted by Granville, the fellow who rode you before,
Across the bleak hills of Monaro, and over the seas to the war,
You flinched not, nor flew from gunfire, you ran at the Turk on the plain,
And now 'tis your master is calling and wanting his waler again.
Old Bill, you remember the thunder, the thrill of your speed, in the race,
The lurch as you rose at the hurdles, to finish the head of the chase;
With Granville far over the withers, with knees pressing into your side,
And you, you could gallop like lightning, and faith, all the Ryries could ride!

Plain Bill, you are over twenty, the nights in the stables seem cold,
You're not quite the same as a yearling, you're broken and stumbling and old:
You veer as you lift at the hurdle, you pant as you rise the hill,
But your heart is the heart of the youngster that galloped through hell-fire with Bill.

Gen. Granville 'Bull' Ryrie mounted on Plain Bill.

Old Bill, 'tis your master calling: he's sick of town and car;
I guess your nostrils will tremble and answer wherever you are;
For Granville of old in the saddle, with hands like a child on the rein –
The two Bills are lonely and homesick, and wanting each other again.

17. Tim – Charles Carter, 8th Light Horse Regiment, Victoria, took part in the charge on Beersheba. He was a jockey and his beloved horse was called Tim. At the end of the war he shot him as he could not bear to see him sent where he would be worked to death.

18. Pie – Col. Arthur Olden led the 10th Light Horse Regiment into Damascus on his faithful mount, Pie. It was Olden and his forces who beat TE Lawrence (Lawrence of Arabia) into Damascus.

19. Banjo – Elijah Conn loved his horse, Banjo, and never forgot him. For the rest of his life, he could not talk about him without tears coming to his eyes. Banjo is the subject of Eric Bogle's famous ballad *As If He Knows*, which is a tribute to the horses that did not come home…

20. Baldy – Corporal Edwin Husband wrote a chapter for a 1919 publication, *Australia in Palestine*, writing the story from the perspective of his horse, Baldy.

21. Horse 920 – A story called 'The Falling Star' told by an Australian trooper was about a new horse allocated to him by the Army Remount Section. Joe Masters was stuck with Horse 920, a crafty and cunning horse. He would trip and stumble at will and also had moon blindness (not good for night marches.) He would crash into well-behaved horses, biting and kicking in parades. He would go backwards, and if Joe tried to stop him, the horse would fall, grunt and roll as if in agony. Joe avoided parades and exercises. Joe was hospitalised and joined the 8th Light Horse after the battle of Gaza and was reallocated another horse, Big Red. No-one knew what had happened to Horse 920. After the battle at Rafa, while resting in an oasis filled with palms and running water, an incident occurred: One night Joe was woken by someone breathing on his face. He woke and yelled in fright. Horse 920, who had been thought lost in the desert, had found Joe. After that, when Joe accepted him as a friend, 920 never fell again, kicked or bit or misbehaved on parade.

22. Dolly – the horse of Herbert Drake, 4th Light Horse Regiment. Dolly was a friend. He gave her a drink of water from his upturned hat and took her out to graze when the opportunity arose. Many troopers shared water with their horses, a phenomenon committed to canvas in the painting 'Sharing His Water' by Ron Marshall of the Light Horse Art Gallery.

23. Bally – Harry Chauvel rode his beloved bay gelding, Bally, to third place in the Anzac Steeplechase at a race meeting in March 1917, organised after the battle at Rafa, just before the first Battle of Gaza. Chauvel knew that events such as organised games and races were crucial for the morale of battle-weary troopers. Chauvel was firm in the principle that the rider should always think of his mount before himself.

24. Songster – A British horse, Songster was one of the oldest and most decorated horses of the First World War. In 1914 he was brought in for the war effort and paraded in Loughborough Market Square in Leicestershire. At fourteen years old and just over fifteen hands, he really was too old and too small, but he was said to have had huge character, intelligence and bravery. He kept himself and his rider, Trooper Bert Main, alive for the duration of the war. Songster could untie himself from the peg during heavy shelling, then come back to Bert when the coast was clear. He died in 1940 at the age of forty years, an incredible age for a horse.

English trooper Bert Main on Songster, 1915.

Bill the Bastard and General Shanahan rest among the palm trees.

Picture: News Ltd

Banjo Paterson (far right) inspects a sulking horse in Egypt.

Australian War Memorial

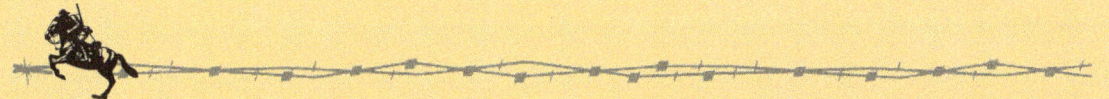

17
Memorials

Memorials are important as they serve as a reminder of the importance of lives (human and, in this case, horse) that have been lost in serving others. These memorial statues are powerful; stirring emotions as you gaze at the likeness and read the inscriptions which have been written with love and admiration. I have included some powerful memorials in Australia and one from New Zealand.

1. Royal Botanic Gardens, Sydney: Horses of the Desert Mounted Corps Memorial

A long bronze relief of three horses with heads hanging low, ammunition pouches around their necks, being led over the sand dunes. It was erected by members of Desert Mounted Corps and friends of the brave horses who carried them over the Sinai Desert into Palestine 1915-1918. It was unveiled by Lady Sibyl Chauvel on Anzac Day 1950. The inscription reads, "They suffered wounds, thirst, hunger and weariness almost beyond endurance but never failed. They did not come home. We will never forget them."

2. Beersheba, Israel: Peter Corlett's statue, Young Digger James

This memorial statue is in the Park of the Australian Soldier, which was opened in Beersheba in 2008. It is a striking bronze sculpture of a horse in full flight while the soldier leans forward into the trench, bayonet in his right hand poised to strike. Businessman Richard Pratt made it a gift to his boyhood friend James, "a better mate than most men could hope for".

3. Tongala, northern Victoria: A monument to 24 Australian Light Horse regiments and their horses

This is a two-metre-tall statue of a horseman carrying an empty saddle, bridle and saddle cloth, walking away, head lowered. Below the statue is the poem, Farewell Old War Horse. This statue is a tribute to 170,000 Australian horses that went overseas.

4. Murrumburrah-Harden, NSW, home of Australia's 1st Light Horse Regiment

A bronze statue titled Retreat from Romani depicts Bill the Bastard carrying Gen. Shanahan and other four troopers to safety at the Battle of Romani, 3 August 1916. While the statue is a tribute, it does not do justice to the incredible act of bravery that Shanahan and Bill undertook. I was disappointed with the representation. This feat is an incredible testament to the bravery of both horse and trooper. For his effort, Shanahan earned the Distinguished Service Order. In 2016, a new life-size statue was erected to honour Bill the Bastard. It stands tall and proud, capturing the essence of the great horse and the bond with his rider.

5. Tamworth: Memorial to Waler Light Horse

This memorial depicts a Light Horseman standing beside his mount. The trooper is saying goodbye to the horse. It is life-size and as you look at it you cannot fail to be moved by the pathos.

6. Albany: the Desert Mounted Corps Memorial

The first convoy of Light Horsemen sailed from Albany, WA. The original memorial to soldiers of the Mounted Desert Corps who were killed in the Sinai and Palestine was unveiled at Port Said, Egypt, in 1932. For 24 years it watched ships pass through the Suez Canal before being irreparably damaged by gunfire during the Suez Crisis in 1956. What could be salvaged was sent to Australia and the pieces arrived in 1960. The masonry was rebuilt and a copy of the original bronze was finally erected at Mt Clarence, Albany, in 1964.

The sculpture depicts an Australian Light Horseman stooping down from the saddle to pick up a New Zealander whose horse has been injured. In this symbolic act of comradeship, the 'Spirit of the Anzac' legend is depicted. It is one of the most powerful of all memorial statues commemorating the service of the mounted forces.

7. Canberra: A second replica Desert Mounted Corps statue

was unveiled in 1968 on Anzac Parade in Canberra. The New Zealand horse Bess (mount of Col. Powles, NZ Rifles) survived the war and was the model for the statue. The body language of the Australian and New Zealander is slightly altered in this replica. It could be said it depicts an Aussie protecting his NZ comrade with his wounded horse or two brothers in arms ready to dismount and engage in battle on foot as they had been trained to do.

8. Canberra: Horse's head on a granite plinth

This is a memorial to animals in war and was erected in 2009 in the grounds of the Australian War Memorial. This horse's head is the only remaining fragment of an original sculpture destroyed by rioters during the Suez Crisis.

9. Kyneton: Monument to Kyneton's Mounted Rifle Troop

A large bronze monument in the police station grounds, Jennings Street. The monument recognises Kyneton's Mounted Rifle Troop. Kyneton, in Victoria, is recognised as the home of the Australian Light Horse, starting with the Kyneton Mounted Rifle Troop of 1859. The memorial is a tribute to the mounted horsemen of the 4th Light Horse Regiment in WW1, many of whom came from Kyneton farms where they grew up with horses. The statue depicts a Victorian trooper on his horse in the Charge at Beersheba. The monument was originally sited at the town's Mechanics Institute as that was the original meeting place of the Kyneton District Mounted Rifle Corps. Unfortunately, the statue was damaged and now resides outside the police station.

10. Maribyrnong, Melbourne: Memorial to all Australian horses killed in conflict

A rendering in metal of Sandy, Major-General Bridges' favourite mount and friend, at Maribyrnong Remount Hill. Sandy is the only Australian war horse to come home and serves as a representative of all of Australia's war horses. The Friends of Sandy group fought tirelessly for this memorial to eventuate. The statue was finally unveiled on 30 October 2017. The permanent memorial will eventually be on site in front of the Fisher Stables in Maribyrnong.

11. Adelaide: War Horse Memorial Drinking Trough, Pinky Park

The trough commemorates the Charge at Beersheba, 31 October 1917.

12. Warrnambool: the Jericho Cup

Leading up to 2018, a Melbourne philanthropist, Bill Gibbons, backed a proposal for the commemoration of 100 years since the end of the 'war to end all wars', on 11 November 1918. The Warrnambool Racing Club staged the inaugural 'Jericho Cup' in 2018 in honour of the Anzacs and the horses they took to war.

A promotional running of the Jericho Cup at Warrnambool in military uniform.

The original Jericho Cup was a race meeting staged to fool the Turks about a pending attack, used as a distraction. The now annual race at Warrnambool is run over 4600 metres—the longest flat race on Australia—as a tribute to a three-mile race that Banjo Paterson and other Light Horse officers staged in Palestine to boost morale. A short-distance race, the Midnight Madness, also takes place in memory of Guy Haydon's horse Midnight, who was one of the fastest horses sent to the war from Australia, as well as the 'Charge of Beersheba Sprint, 1000m.

I attended the 6th race meet, on 3/11/23 and was overwhelmed by the spirit and tributes to the Light Horse. Bill Gibbons spoke about his delight at the support this event has received. This race meet is growing in stature and I was honoured to be able to be part of it.

13. Otahuhu, South Auckland, New Zealand: Soldier Memorial

This is a life-size bronze of an 8th Auckland Rifleman seated on his horse which is rearing up because it has been startled by shellfire. It is a magnificent statue.

14. Bulls, North Island, New Zealand: private memorial

Stone headstone for Bess, Col. Powles' faithful mount who served with him for the entire Desert Campaign. She and three others were the only NZ horses to return home after serving time in quarantine in England. It is a modest memorial for an exceptional horse.

15. Tzemach, Israel: The Aborigine and his Horse

This statue was erected in a ceremony on 25 September 2019 at Tzemach (formerly in Palestine) where a short, fierce battle began at dawn on 25 September 1918—the last charge of the Light Horse. The sculpture depicts trooper Jack Pollard holding a bible and bending over the grave of one of his brothers in arms. The horse is bending over the grave also. It is a moving tribute to honour all First Nations soldiers who served in WWI. It is the first memorial to acknowledge the contribution that First Nations people made in the war effort. Back in Australia at the time of World War I they were not considered Australian citizens and could not vote. The 11th Regiment from Queensland, who fought in this battle, had 30 First Nations troopers, the largest number serving in one unit.

16. Melbourne: Water trough, Shrine of Remembrance

A grey granite horse-trough memorial constructed in 1926 to mark the contribution of horses in Australia's battles, erected by the Purple Cross Society of Victoria. The Purple Cross, formed in 1915, was an organisation of women animal lovers who were concerned about the welfare of troop horses sent overseas. Their fundraising efforts raised money to supply bandages, medicine and 'comforts' for the horses. It meant a great deal to the troops when they saw how their horses and mules were cared for. Veterinary supplies were meagre and the wounds suffered by many horses would have been horrific. The society erected the trough in St Kilda Road; it was moved in 1987 to the grounds of the Shrine of Remembrance. The inscription reads:

> *A Tribute to our war horses.*
> *He gains no crosses as a soldier may,*
> *No medals for the many risks he runs*
> *He only in his puzzled way*
> *Sticks to his guns!*

It is said that this epitaph speaks directly to a war horse called David, who served in Britain's 107 Battery Regiment 1899-1902 during the Boer War and then as a 'wheeler' in a gun team in France in WW1. He saw out his final days at a rest home for old horses in England where he died in 1921. Had he been a soldier he would have qualified for the Queen's Medal with four clasps; King's Medal with two clasps; the 1914 Star with bar; War, Victory and Long Service Medals; and had four wound stripes.

18. Dipso

An article was published in a family history magazine and broadcast on the ABC in 2018 about a man named Pat Gallagher, who was determined to keep the memory of the amazing war horses alive. He was looking at the memorial in Macquarie Street, Sydney, when he noticed a wreath made of oats lying on the ground and a card bearing the name 'Dipso'. He was intrigued by the name, as it was an old term for an alcoholic and the image of a drunken horse stuck with him; because a wreath had been laid for him, Gallagher

Dipso, Palestine, November 1916.

went on to find out about Dipso. He discovered that he was an ex-thoroughbred racehorse from NSW. His owner, Reginald Roy Brown, bought the horse because he wanted to ride the best horse to war. Brown enlisted in the 6th Light Horse Regiment and on December 1915 they left Sydney bound for Egypt. Brown served at Gallipoli, became ill and was evacuated to a hospital in England. He later accepted a commission into the UK Royal Field Artillery and never saw his horse again.

Dipso was given to his friend, commanding officer Captain Stuart Archibald Tooth, and was used by him for the rest of the Desert Campaign. He was part of the Battle of Romani and later the battle of Gaza. After the eventual capture of Gaza, the British decided to celebrate. They held a race meeting on the battleground where the 'Gaza Cup' was the main attraction. Dipso, ridden by the now-promoted Major Archibald Tooth, won easily. Dipso was involved in four different fronts of war. Only eighteen horses out of 520 originally allocated to the 6th Regiment survived without casualty. Obviously, this horse had many adventures and faced many dangers but luckily for him, he ended up in the Indian Cavalry, known for its fair treatment of horses.

What astonished Gallagher even more was that twenty years later, he was at the Anzac Parade Desert Mounted Corps Memorial at the Australian War Memorial when he noticed a small wreath made from oats and a card with 'DIPSO' written on it. This horse was still being remembered ... Could it have been from the Brown family who had a photo of Dipso take pride of place in three generations?

The words, "We will never forget them," take on special poignancy in this instance when we know that they applied specifically to a much-loved horse.

19. Julia Creek, Queensland: Spirit of the Light Horse

This sculpture stands next to the Julia Creek RSL in McKinlay Shire, north-west Queensland. It is a life-size horseman mounted on his horse, with a backdrop of laser-cut steel silhouettes representing Light Horsemen charging into battle. Created by Sue Tilley and made from scraps of metal collected locally, it was opened on Anzac Day 2015. The "poppy and Shellal mosaic" path on which the horse and rider stand was added in 2018 – artist, Claudia Williams.

20. Seville, Victoria: Four-metre glass panel in memory of local former 4th Light Horseman George Cassidy

This memorial was opened on Anzac Day 2021 at Seville in Victoria's Yarra Valley. It is an image of Cassidy, aged 16, just after he enlisted, along with a letter he wrote home describing being in an attack.

21. Seymour, Victoria: Plaque in the Australian Light Horse Memorial Park

General Allenby wrote, "The Australian Light Horse proved equal to the best. He has earned the gratitude of the Empire and the admiration of the world."

22. Bonnie Doon, Victoria: Memorial and plaque

A statue of a digger and close by a plaque, beside a pine tree. The plaque reads, "This tree, Pinus halepensis, has been propagated from the original Lone Pine of Gallipoli. It memorialises Trooper Stephen Arbuthnot, No. 876, 8th Light Horse Regiment, native of Bonnie Doon. He landed at Gallipoli on 5th August 1915 and was killed two days later during a suicidal charge at the Nek, along with some 465 members of his unit."

A recent short trip I took from Bonnie Doon down through Seymour in Victoria overwhelmed me with how real and sad these young men's lives were. It was only by chance that I noticed the memorial at Bonnie Doon, a town that was swamped by the construction of the huge Eildon Weir. It may well be that young Stephen Arbuthnot was one of those young, enthusiastic boys who jumped on the train with his horse to train at Seymour down the line. I visited the Australian Light Horse Memorial Park at Seymour on my way home from Bonnie Doon. As I stood in 'the Waler's paddock,' I could almost hear the thundering hooves and enthusiastic yells from excited young men as they trained. Maybe young Stephen trained here before heading off on the train to Melbourne and then being shipped to Egypt. He landed in Gallipoli and two days later, was dead.

Men of the 8th Light Horse Regiment became soldiers at Seymour before sacrificing themselves in the disastrous attack on 'The Nek' on 7 August 1915.

Some of the men who rode into history at the Charge of Beersheba in October 1917 first passed through the Seymour Camp.

Appendix

WHO'S WHO IN LEADERSHIP

COMMANDERS

British Leaders

The British commanders had the authority to direct the war effort and had little regard for Australian know-how.

Lieutenant-General Sir William Birdwood. In charge of all Australian operations. A British officer who was popular and friendly. He led the Australian Light Horse at Gallipoli.

Lieutenant-General Sir Archibald Murray. Commander in Chief, Egyptian Expeditionary Force. British officer in charge of the Desert Campaign and formed the Desert Column, in charge 1916 to June 1917. He directed the campaign from headquarters in Cairo and had no real understanding of the situation in the desert.

General Sir Edmund Allenby. Commander June 1917 to November 1918. British officer who took over from Murray in June 1917 after the disastrous Gaza defeats of the Greater Mounted Force. He renamed the mounted force the Desert Corps. He directed the war from the actual camps in the area.

Lieutenant General Sir Phillip Chetwode. Desert Column 1916 to 1917. In charge of three British Divisions. He prepared the plans for the attack on Beersheba, the mounted troops by the east, infantry attacking from the south-west, and made sure the Turks and Germans thought the main attack was on Gaza.

Australian Leaders

Major-General Sir William Throsby Bridges. Commander of the Australian 1st division, AIF, the first ashore at Gallipoli.

Lt-General Sir Harry Chauvel. Early in 1916 General Chauvel, who had commanded the First Light Horse Brigade, was given the task of organising the Anzac Mounted Division defending the Suez Canal, 1916 to 1917, and then the Desert Mounted Corps, 1917 to 1918. He was the only Australian to be given the huge responsibility of conducting the desert war. He was responsible for the victory at Romani, the first of the desert campaign, and the Beersheba charge in which the Australian Light Horse captured the wells needed to water the horses and turned the campaign to success after other complex and difficult battles culminating in the capture of Damascus.

Lt-Colonel Murray William James Bourchier. Leader of the 4th regiment, Victoria, who charged at full gallop over two miles into Turkish entrenchments and further into Beersheba to secure water. He also commanded a joint force of 4 and 12 Light Horse Regiments in the final advance into Damascus.

Brigadier-General William Grant. Leader of the 4th Light Horse Brigade and the two regiments who charged Beersheba.

Major-General Sir Granville Ryrie. A great Australian bushman who was a distinguished Light Horse commander. A veteran of the Boer War in South Africa, he organised the 2nd Light Horse Brigade and led the troops in Sinai and Palestine. A shrewd commander.

Lt-General Sir John Monash. Australian in charge of infantry at the Western Front. He was the only Australian officer to be given such a huge contingent. He was responsible for victory on the Western Front.

New Zealand Leaders

Brigadier-General Edward Chaytor. Commanded the New Zealand Mounted Rifles which included the Auckland, Canterbury and Wellington Rifles Regiments, from December 1915 to April 1917. He then took command of the ANZAC Mounted Division, 1917 to 1918, when General Chauvel was appointed to command all the cavalry. He was proficient, quiet and thorough in his leadership.

Colonel Guy Powles. Recorded events in his diaries and took many photos.

Glossary

Artillery	Heavy guns worked by a group and pulled by a team of draughthorses
AIF	Australian Imperial Force. Infantry and mounted
ALH	Australian Light Horse. Mounted force
'barcoo polish'	Colloquial term for a shortcut method of categorising a horse as broken in. Force the horse into a stock race in a yard. A rider jumps on his back for a couple of minutes. The horse has been ridden
bayonet	long blade fixed to a rifle for use in close, hand-to-hand fighting
berseem	Alexandria berseem clover, a forage crop for horses to eat, often compared to alfalfa
Billjims	ordinary Australian soldiers
bird's eye	type of seed for horses to eat
bivouac	a temporary camp without cover
brackish water	slightly salty water
breeches	short trousers fastened below the knee and worn for riding
buck jumper	a bucking horse with bad habits
bully beef	corned beef in a tin (often referred to as dog food by troopers)
cacolet	stretcher or chair fitted to the sides of a camel to carry wounded solders from battle

Cameleer	trooper who rode a camel
Campaign	a series of military operations with a set purpose, usually in one area
charger	cavalry horse
corps	an army unit
Desert Column	mounted forces (on horseback)
Desert Corps	mounted forces renamed in June 1917
Despatch riders	riders sent on horses to deliver urgent messages
Devils on horses	term used by Turks for the ANZAC riders because of their ability to move swiftly.
draught horse	a heavy horse breed used for pulling heavy loads
En-Zeds	New Zealanders
fanatis	containers made of copper or tin used to carry water on camels
Field ambulance	Mobile medical unit equipped to provide first aid to soldiers while still in sight of battle. They were crucial as they followed the mounted troops
Fly fringes	made of cord and attached to horses' brow bands to keep flies off eyes
Gun wheel	Six to twelve horses were required to pull heavy guns on carts for the offensive in France
hooshters	colloquial term for camels in the AIF
'Horse dung Hussars'	A. B. Paterson called the older men this in the Remount Unit. Hussars were a medieval light cavalry from Hungary; fierce and brave
horse lines	horses tied along a long line when at camp
HRU – Horse Retrieval Unit	Sent to pick up wounded soldiers and dead horses
Imperial Army	British Army

infantry	Soldiers who fight on foot with rifles
Jackos	Australian troops' nickname for Turks
Kangaroo Feathers	Turkish nickname for the Australians because of the emu feathers worn in their hats
Khamsin winds	fierce, dry desert winds
Kings of the Feather	Australians — another term used by the Turks
mealies	corn mash for horses
'Methusaliers'	affectionate term used at Remount Depot by AB Paterson for the older men employed as grooms
'My Corps Cavalry'	Gen. Monash affectionately called the 13th Light Horse regiment this as they served on Western Front
nadi	river bed
occupy	take control of a place by military conquest
outlaws	horses with bad habits, eg bucking
palm hods	small hollows between hills—often with stale water and date palms. Gave some shade from the fierce heat
'Patent self-emptiers'	jokey term used for slippery army saddles
platoon	part of a company, two or more sections
puttees	strips of cloth wound around the lower leg for protection and support
'Queensland black watch'	First Nations troopers of 8th Light Horse
race	narrow corral in stockyards, used to restrict stock movements
rough riders	rodeo riders who ride buck jumpers
reconnaissance/ reconnoitre	military observation of an area
redoubt	a small mound – defensive position. Can have machine guns set up

remount	horse trained for military service, a replacement
Sand cart	hand-made device for ambulance in the desert to transport the wounded
sapper	private soldier in engineering or survey corps of an army
signaller	person working in military communications
slouch hat	Australians' hat with a soft wide brim
strangles	infectious disease in horses causing blockages in air passages
Taube	type of enemy plane
tibbin	inferior local chaff contaminated with dust
Tommies	English soldiers
trooper	soldier in mounted force
'trucks of the desert'	camels, which were used to haul large loads
wadi	watercourse that is dry, except in the rainy season
Waler	Australian breed of stock horse
'Well and Trulies'	Australian nickname for the Wellington Mounted Rifles
White Gurkhas	Australians: Turks viewed them as good fighters. Gurkhas were Nepalese soldiers in the British Army. Their motto, 'better to die than be a coward.'
Willy willy	a whirlwind or dust storm
yeomanry	volunteer cavalry units in the British Army

Timeline of Middle East Campaign

1914
28 July: war is declared in Europe.
December: Australian and New Zealand troops arrive in Egypt.

1915 GALLIPOLI
9 April: AIF sent to Gallipoli. Horses left in Egypt.
25 April: First Anzacs land at Gallipoli.
12 May: Light Horse lands at Gallipoli.
7 August: Light Horse fight in the bloody battle of the Nek.
19-20 December: Last troops evacuated from Gallipoli.

1916 SINAI DESERT
1916: Sir Archibald Murray Commander in Chief of the Egyptian Expeditionary Force.
15 March: Formation of Anzac Mounted Division and Imperial Mounted Division. They formed the Desert Column with Harry Chauvel as commander.
April: Light Horse Brigades ordered to protect the Suez Canal from Turkish forces.
May-June-July: Summer. Light Horse required to search for Turkish troops and chase. Sinai Desert.
3 to 5 August: Defeat Turks at Battle of Romani—first major Light Horse battle in the Sinai. Eighty-kilometre march to El Arish on coast and Magdhaba, inland.
20 December: Captured El Arish, Sinai Desert. Second battle.
23 December: Captured Magdhaba, Sinai. Third battle. Winter; bitter cold, rain.
25 December: Christmas. Victory celebrations. Parade Turkish Flag. Two weeks' march.

1917 PALESTINE
9 January: Capture Rafa (on coast) Border of Palestine/Sinai.

Palestine: Murray organises forces into the Desert Column. March through Palestine, Holy Land, through the Judean Hills to Gaza, stronghold on high ground.
26 March: Failure of first attempt to capture Gaza, Palestine.
17-19 April: Failure of second attempt to capture Gaza.
28 June: Allenby took over from Murray. Reorganised forces into the Desert Corps. Harry Chauvel in charge.

ISRAEL
Summer. Heat.
Five-month gridlock from Gaza (coast) to Beersheba (inland) Turkish Defensive Line.
31 October: Charged Beersheba. Captured wells and allowed for the capture of Gaza. History's last successful cavalry charge.
Gaza-Beersheba Line broken.
Winter. Worst in years. Heavy rains.
Two-month push to Jerusalem, Palestine. Capture the Holy City.
7-9 December: Enter Jerusalem.
11 December: General Allenby enters Jerusalem on foot.
25 December: Christmas, cold and wet.

1918 JORDAN AND SYRIA
SYRIA
Jan/Feb/March: Jordan Valley. Cold and miserable.
21 February: Capture Jericho.
22 March: Light Horse start battles at Es Salt and Amman in Jordan.
2 May: Capture Es Salt.
June/July/August: Summer in Jordan Valley.
September to November: the Great Ride. Advance to Damascus, Syria.
19-22 September: Capture Jaffa (on the coast)
25 September: Capture Amman.
9 October: ALH first to Damascus. Turks surrender.
11 November: Armistice. End WW1.

Light Horse formations and leaders

The Light Horse was not a cavalry as the men did not fight with sword and lance. They were called Mounted Infantry in Queensland, Western Australia and Tasmania. They were called Mounted Rifles in NSW, Victoria and South Australia, and fought with rifle and bayonet.

Section = 4 men

Troop = 8 sections = 32 men.

Squadron = 4 troops, 128 men. Horses in Squadron A, chestnuts. Squadron B, bays and light brown and Squadron C, dark brown.

Regiment = 3-4 squadrons = 600-plus men. Led by a Lieutenant-Colonel.

Brigade = 3-plus regiments = 2500 – 5000 men. Brigadier-General.

Division = 3-4 brigades = 7000 – 8000 men. Major-General.

Corps = 2 or more divisions = 30,000-plus men. Lieutenant-General.

The Australian Light Horse had 5 Brigades at the end of 1918.

The Middle East Push
The Commander in chief of the Egyptian Expeditionary Forces was Sir Edmund Murray, 1916 to June 1917. He formed the Desert Column in January 1917. Sir Philip Chetwode was the commander. The column consisted of:

Light Horse formations and leaders

1 The Anzac Mounted Division, led by Harry Chauvel, consisting of the 1st and 2nd Brigades and the NZ Mounted Rifles. 1916-1917.

2 Imperial Mounted Division, January 1917, led by Major-General HW Hodgson, consisting of the 3rd and 4th Brigades and 2 Yeomanry.

Sir Edmund Murray had been replaced as leader of the Egyptian Expeditionary Forces by Sir Edmund Allenby in June 1917. He needed to restructure the format of the mounted cavalry. This mounted force became the Desert Corps in July 1917. Australia's Harry Chauvel was promoted leader of this organisation. The Corps consisted of:

1 Anzac Mounted Division, led by Chaytor, consisting of 1st Brigade, 2nd Brigade and NZ Mounted Rifles 1917-1918 and then by Brigadier-General Granville Ryrie 1918-1919.

2 Australian Mounted Division, led by Major General H. W. Hodgson, consisting of the 3rd, 4th and 5th Light Horse Brigade.

It is to be noted that First Nations men were not initially allowed to join the Australian Light Horse, but in 1917 mixed-race First Nations men could enlist. It has been recorded that 1000 First Nations men enlisted, mostly from Queensland.

BRIGADES	LEADER	BATTLES

Brigade commanders changed during the war.

BRIGADES	LEADER	BATTLES
1st Brigade 1 Regiment, NSW 2 Regiment, Qld 3 Regiment. SA & TAS.	Brig-General Charles Cox ('Fighting Charlie')	Romani
2nd Brigade 5 Regiment, Qld 6 Regiment, NSW 7 Regiment, NSW	Brig-General Granville Ryrie ('Old Brig')	Romani
3rd Brigade 8 Regiment, Vic 9 Regiment, SA & Vic 10 Regiment, WA	Brigadier. Gen. John Royston ('Galloping Jack')	Romani and Palestine

4th Brigade 4 Regiment, Vic Colonel Murray	Brig-Gen. William Grant, then Lt. Burchier	Beersheba, Jerusalem
11 Regiment, Qld and SA 12 Regiment, NSW 13 Regiment, Vic, sent to Western Front.		Es Salt and Damascus
5th Brigade	B.G. George Onslow/ Lt-Colonel Donald C. Cameron	
14 Regiment, Imperial Camel Corps 15 Regiment, Imperial Camel Corps French Colonial Regiment.		Plain of Sharon
New Zealand Mounted Rifles	Brig-General Andrew Russell, 1914–1915; Major-Gen Edward Chaytor, 1915–1917; Brig-General William Meldrum, 1917–1919.	
Auckland MR Regiment Wellington MR Regiment Canterbury MR Regiment		

Commanders changed frequently and it is hard to always have an accurate reference.

I am not a military historian so all facts are not detailed. This is not meant to be a detailed military history. My passion is an understanding of the amazing close partnership between man and horse which has been revealed in this bloody conflict. I marvel at their efforts and am in awe of those magnificent creatures who remained loyal unto death.

Regiments and troopers mentioned

4th Light Horse Regiment, Victoria. Motto: 'Endure and fight.' 540 men. Three or four squadrons. Formed at Broadmeadows Military Camp, August, 1914. Two squadrons sent to the Western Front. 'I serve.' Brigadier Murray Bourchier from Strathmerton, central Victoria, was their leader. They were in the charge at Beersheba.

5th Light Horse Regiment, Queensland. Motto: 'The best.' They fought in all conflicts since Gallipoli. Ion Idriess, author of *The Desert Column*, served in this regiment. Maxwell Curwen Walker, cousin of my grandfather, Ronald Curwen Walker, also served in this regiment. He was born in Deniliquin, NSW, in 1891 and became a station overseer at Longreach, Queensland.

8th Light Horse Regiment, Victoria. Motto: 'The Fighting Eighth.' Formed at Broadmeadows, September 1914. 550 men. They were decimated at the Nek, Gallipoli. 47 of the 550 returned. Sergeant George Auchterlonie from Narracan in Gippsland, who took his horse, Paddy, to war, trooper 'Snow' Matson and William (Bill) Griffiths, who wrote a letter to me, were in this regiment.

10th Light Horse Regiment, WA. Motto: 'Strike and strike swiftly.' This regiment was also decimated at the Nek, Gallipoli. Hugo Throssell of this regiment won a VC for his bravery at the Nek. Regiment also involved in the first and second failed assaults on Gaza, and the entry into Jerusalem. Lt-Colonel Arthur Olden led them to be the first into Damascus.

12th Light Horse Regiment, NSW. Motto: 'Fortune is the companion of valour.' Guy Haydon and his horse, Midnight, were with this regiment and were part of the Beersheba charge.

13th Light Horse Regiment, Victoria. Motto: 'The Devil's Own.' Sent to the front in France with two squadrons of the 4th: Motto: 'Loyal 'til death.'

LEST WE FORGET

Bibliography

Auchterlonie, Gloria, *Dad's War Stuff: The Diaries of George Auchterlonie*, Pazzaz Printing, Morwell, Victoria, 2001

Australian Light Horse, Education resources, Commonwealth of Australia, 2013

Bain, Evan, 'No good at all', Oral History, 10th Light Horse Regiment. State Library of Western Australia

Balsarini, Martin, *Hell or Beersheba*, Documentary. Eye witness account by Balsarini, of Chiltern, Victoria, machine gunner in Victorian Light Horse Regiment

Baly, Lindsay. *Horseman, Pass By. The Australian Light Horse in WW1*. Kangaroo Press, Australia, 2003

Bradley, Phillip, *Australian Light Horse*, Allen & Unwin, 2016

Brocker, Susan, *Brave Bess and the ANZAC Horses*, Harper Collins NZ, 2010

Cameron, David W. *The Charge: The Australian Light Horse Victory at Beersheba*, Viking 2017

Cleland, Fran, 'Walers left adrift,' *Weekly Times*, 28 December 2011

Coultard-Clark, Chris, 'One came home,' *Wartime*, official magazine of Australian War Memorial 1990-2002

Daley, Paul, *Beersheba*, Melbourne University Press, 2009

Garnett, Michael P, *Kyneton Mounted Rifle Corps*. Historical Publications, Romsey, Vic, 2013

'Gisborne Soldiers Welcomed,' *Gisborne Gazette*, Victoria, August 1919

Gullett et al (eds), *Australia in Palestine*, Angus & Robertson Ltd, 1919

Hamilton (Duchess of), Jill, *First to Damascus: The story of the Great Ride and Lawrence of Arabia*, Kangaroo Press, 2002

Hamilton, Jill, *From Gallipoli to Gaza: The desert poets of WW1*, Simon & Schuster Australia, 2003

Hamilton, John, *Goodbye Cobber, God Bless You*, Macmillan, 2004

Hamilton, John, *The Prince of Valour*, Macmillan, Sydney, 2012

Heard, Barry, *Tag*, Scribe Publications, 2009

Howells, John (prepared by), December 2007 https://www.lancers.org.au/site/Light_Horse_France.php

Idriess, Ion, *The Desert Column: Leaves from the diary of an Australian trooper in Gallipoli, Sinai and Palestine*, Angus & Robertson, Sydney, 1951

Jones, Ian, *Australia at War: The Light Horse*, Hodder Australia series, 1986

Kent, David A, *The Australian Remount Unit in Egypt 1915–1919: A footnote to history*, Journal of Australian War Memorial 1, 1982.

Kia Ora Coo-ee, magazine for the Anzacs in the Middle East, various months, 1918

King, Johnathan, *Palestine Diaries: The Light Horsemen's own story, battle by battle*, Scribe Publications, Victoria, 2017

King, Johnathan. *Gallipoli Diaries: The Anzacs' own story day by day*, Kangaroo Press, NSW, 2003

Kinloch, Terry, *Devils on Horses—In the words of ANZACS in the Middle East 1916-19*. Exisle Publishing, Auckland, 2012

Maurstad, Anita; Davis, Dona and Cowles, Sarah. 2013. 'Co-being and intra-action in horse-human relationships: A multi-species ethnography of be(com)ing human and be(com)ing horse.' Social Anthropology. 21. 10.1111/1469-8676.12029

Mitchell, Elyne *Light Horse: The story of Australia's mounted troops*, Macmillan Australia, 1978

Olden, Arthur (Lt-Col), *Westralian Cavalry in the War*, comprehensive history of the 10th Light Horse Regiment AIF

Paterson, A B, *Happy Dispatches*, Lansdowne Press, Sydney, 1981

Perry, Roland. *Bill the Bastard. The story of Australia's Greatest War Horse*, Allen & Unwin, 2012

Perry, Roland, *The Australian Light Horse*, Hachette, Australia, 2010

Rome, Stephen, 'Beersheba, legend of the Light Horse', *Weekend Australian*, October 28–29, 2017

Ryan, Kelly, 'Brave War Horse', *Herald Sun*, 24 April, 2009

Seely, Jack (Gen.) *Warrior*, 1934

Wikipedia entry, 'Waler Horse'.

Youl, Robyn & Hallett, Keith, *From Desk to Dugout: The Education of a Victorian Anzac*, Brolga Publishing Pty Ltd, Melbourne, Victoria, 2015

Returning to camp.